P9-CEP-952

A FACTORY of ONE

Applying Lean Principles to Banish Waste
and Improve Your Personal Performance

A FACTORY of ONE

Applying Lean Principles to Banish Waste
and Improve Your Personal Performance

Daniel Markovitz

CRC Press
Taylor & Francis Group
Boca Raton   London   New York

CRC Press is an imprint of the
Taylor & Francis Group, an **informa** business

A PRODUCTIVITY PRESS BOOK

CRC Press
Taylor & Francis Group
6000 Broken Sound Parkway NW, Suite 300
Boca Raton, FL 33487-2742

© 2012 by Taylor & Francis Group, LLC
CRC Press is an imprint of Taylor & Francis Group, an Informa business

No claim to original U.S. Government works

Printed in the United States of America on acid-free paper
Version Date: 20111102

International Standard Book Number: 978-1-4398-5993-3 (Paperback)

This book contains information obtained from authentic and highly regarded sources. Reasonable efforts have been made to publish reliable data and information, but the author and publisher cannot assume responsibility for the validity of all materials or the consequences of their use. The authors and publishers have attempted to trace the copyright holders of all material reproduced in this publication and apologize to copyright holders if permission to publish in this form has not been obtained. If any copyright material has not been acknowledged please write and let us know so we may rectify in any future reprint.

Except as permitted under U.S. Copyright Law, no part of this book may be reprinted, reproduced, transmitted, or utilized in any form by any electronic, mechanical, or other means, now known or hereafter invented, including photocopying, microfilming, and recording, or in any information storage or retrieval system, without written permission from the publishers.

For permission to photocopy or use material electronically from this work, please access www.copyright.com (http://www.copyright.com/) or contact the Copyright Clearance Center, Inc. (CCC), 222 Rosewood Drive, Danvers, MA 01923, 978-750-8400. CCC is a not-for-profit organization that provides licenses and registration for a variety of users. For organizations that have been granted a photocopy license by the CCC, a separate system of payment has been arranged.

Trademark Notice: Product or corporate names may be trademarks or registered trademarks, and are used only for identification and explanation without intent to infringe.

Library of Congress Cataloging-in-Publication Data

Markovitz, Daniel .
    A factory of one : applying lean principles to banish waste and improve your personal performance / Daniel Markovitz.
       p. ; cm.
    Includes bibliographical references and index.
    Summary: "The same Lean principles that are helping hospitals eliminate waste and improve efficiencies are applicable to individuals working in healthcare. This book not only provides the tools to alleviate the obvious symptoms of inefficiency but also demonstrates how to find the root causes underlying that inefficiency. It presents a practical, step-by-step approach to applying Lean principles to individuals, including real-world examples that illustrate how these principles have been applied in the healthcare industry"--Provided by publisher.
    ISBN 978-1-4398-5993-3 (softcover)
    1. Industrial efficiency. 2. Medical care. I. Title. II. Series.
    [DNLM: 1. Health Personnel--organization & administration. 2. Delivery of Health Care--economics. 3. Efficiency, Organizational. 4. Quality Assurance, Health Care--methods. W 21]

RA399.A1M3678 2012
610.68--dc23   2011026410

Visit the Taylor & Francis Web site at
http://www.taylorandfrancis.com

and the CRC Press Web site at
http://www.crcpress.com

For Lynn, whose love and unwavering
faith is a beacon to me, always.

Acknowledgments

I owe deep debts to the following people, without whom this book would have been impossible:

First and foremost, to my mother and father, who have given me the unparalleled luxury of being able to follow my passions.

To Mark Graban, Kevin Meyer, and Kirk Paluska, who have served as my lean senseis (as hackneyed a phrase as that is) for several years now—and who were stuck with the thankless task of reading early drafts.

To Joe Ely, Bob Emiliani, and Mark Jaben, who were gracious enough to allow me to tell their stories. I hope I did their work justice.

And finally, to Tom Ehrenfeld, whose nagging questions, suggestions, and inspired editing elevated this book from a series of half-baked ideas clumsily stapled together. Even from the beginning, he saw this whole project more clearly than I ever did.

Thank you all.

Contents

Introduction

Imagine being more productive, more efficient, less stressed, and more successful in your work.

Imagine achieving this without a brain transplant, a mastery of office politics on the order of J. Pierrepont Finch, or a raft of assistants ministering to your needs.

Bear with me for a moment for a brief digression about the auto industry. In 1986, it took General Motors 40 hours to make a car, with an average of 13 defects per car. At that same time, Toyota could produce an equivalent car in 18 hours with only 4.5 defects per car. Fast forward to today, and you'll find industry reports showing that GM has now equaled the top manufacturers in efficiency.

What enabled Toyota to outperform GM so remarkably in 1986? What was behind the incredible quality improvement at GM since that time? Fancy robots? Government bailouts? Positive thinking and expensive team-building retreats? Actually, none of these. (Okay, well maybe two—but they are not the real reason.) No, over the past two decades GM and virtually every other manufacturing company that still matters has made profound gains in their operations by adopting a fundamentally different approach to making things. It's called Lean production.

Forget what you may have heard about Lean methods being something that only belongs on the factory floor. In the past decade, pharmaceutical firms, hospitals, banks, insurance companies—even Starbucks—have adopted Lean tools to improve quality and lower costs. In fact, over the past half-century, Lean has proven to be the only system that reliably enables companies to increase output and quality while reducing the required resources. (Toyota actually developed its Lean production system specifically in response to its nearly nonexistent resources in the wake of World War II.)

I believe that this system can bring you, individually, the same benefits.

Because while Lean has enabled companies to make huge gains in how they get things done, there is a new and vast frontier still waiting to be improved: the daily world of individual work. Your work—the work of product development, of advertising sales, of marketing, of human resources benefits management, whatever—the work you do in these functions can be transformed. By applying Lean principles to your work, right now, you can reduce the effort and frenzy that characterize your days and get more, higher-quality work done with less stress.

Lean is not a panacea for all problems, of course. Your boss may still be taking leadership lessons from Bill Lumburgh in the movie *Office Space*. Your company may still have broken processes, silly policies, and antiquated software. But if you learn and adopt a basic set of Lean principles, you'll foster a new mindset that will enable you to see your work differently, do it better, and start on a path of constant improvement and learning in the process.

There are several reasons I'm so passionate about this approach to productivity—but the most important might be that it works. These ideas are not just a collection of inspirational stories or vague exhortations designed to inspire you to "work smarter, not harder." Has anyone ever explained how to work smarter, not harder? What does that mean, anyway?

A Factory of One

Journalist Charles Fishman once explained how a Toyota factory only *looks* like a car factory: "It's really a big brain—a kind of laboratory focused on a single mission: not how to make cars, but how to make cars better." He went on to explain that at Toyota,

> The work is really threefold: making cars, making cars better, and teaching everyone how to make cars better. At its Olympian best, Toyota adds one more level: It is always looking to improve the process by which it improves all the other processes.

In my opinion, this is the core of Lean: the development of awareness and problem-solving skills, the capacity for self-correction, and total dedication to improvement.

The same Lean principles that a company like Toyota uses to eliminate waste and improve the efficiency of processes are also applicable to you as an individual. Just like a factory, you process raw materials (information) to produce something of value to your customers. My contention is that, as the title of this book suggests, you are a factory of one—a small factory, to be sure, occupying only one office chair, but a factory nonetheless. Consequently, key Lean concepts such as 5S, flow, visual management, and standard work all apply to your individual work. Moreover, the application of these concepts at the individual level results in the same kind of benefits: greater efficiency, less waste, and improved focus on customer value. More significantly, learning how to apply these principles to your own work enhances the capabilities that lie at the core of Lean: the development of self-awareness, powerful problem-solving techniques, and the capacity for self-improvement.

These are vague generalities. Let's look at a concrete example: What do 5S and flow (two Lean terms that I'll explain further) mean for a lawyer, for example? An attorney I worked with at a major Silicon Valley firm claimed that, as a partner, business development was his number one priority. Unfortunately, due to client demands, he spent very little time actually doing any business development. He spent the vast majority of his days enslaved by his e-mail inbox. And, even if he could have unshackled himself from his Blackberry, he couldn't find his essential business development files; they were buried under a pile of useless and unused files against the far wall of his office. I'm guessing that you've probably experienced a similar situation and similar frustrations.

What did we do? We applied 5S principles so that he could quickly find the tools and information he needed for business development. We created flow for the repetitive and predictable business development activities, rather than allowing it to be relegated to something that he did "when he had the time." The result? Less stress, greater focus on critical activities, and a huge increase in time spent devoted to business development—which, remember, was his number one priority.

By the way: That's what it means to work smarter, not harder.

With the economy in a severe downturn and stubbornly high unemployment, all institutions—for profit, nonprofit, and government—and all individuals in those institutions need to become more efficient. There's less money in the budget and fewer people to do the work. At the same time, technological advances in communication (e-mail, instant messaging, wikis, Twitter, and so on), combined with increasing organizational complexity, are making both personal and institutional productivity more challenging.

Hmm ... This Sounds Vaguely Familiar

Some of the concepts you'll read about in these pages will be familiar if you've read books by David Allen, Stephen Covey,

Julie Morgenstern, or the host of other efficiency experts. The truth is that telling you not to check e-mail all the time is not exactly a Copernican insight. And telling you that a clean desk is a good idea is something that your mothers almost certainly pounded into you as a kid. In fact, many of the prescriptions are painfully obvious.

And yet.

There's a reason that people (and organizations) still are not implementing these concepts. Providing the tools for improvement just isn't enough. If it were, the plethora of diet books out there touting sensible weight loss tools would actually result in far fewer obese people waddling around with a Twinkie in one hand and a Coke in the other. The painful reality is that most people need something more to help them overcome their natural tendencies toward chaos and inefficiency. Entropy.

More importantly, you also need to know how to find the root causes creating that inefficiency—and eliminate them.

The goal of this book is to help you work more mindfully—to be aware of what you're doing in the moment because you've been able to remove the physical and psychic clutter that dilutes your productivity. The book will teach principles and tools that help you structure how you do your work so that you can identify the best approach—one that helps you get more done, and done better, consistently. You will learn how to make the best practice, common practice.

And while this may sound paradoxical, by analyzing how you process your work and creating systems around your work processes, this book will enable you to stop thinking about *how* you are doing your work so that you can just *do* the work itself.

If you're harried, frazzled, and looking for a way to gain control over the overwhelming demands on your time, you should read this book. The mixture of "what to do" combined with "why to do it" will help you understand the rationale behind the tools. This mixture will also help you modify the ideas to suit the idiosyncrasies of your work situation and your personality. Whether or not you have a background in Lean or work for a manufacturing company, you'll be able to deploy the tools to do your job better, faster, and with less stress—because you are a factory of one.

Let's get going.

Chapter 1

What's Your Job?

> In short, Lean thinking is Lean, because it provides
> a way to do more and more with less and less—less
> human effort, less equipment, less time, and less
> space—while coming closer and closer to providing
> customers with exactly what they want.
>
> **—Jim Womack and Daniel Jones,**
> ***Lean Thinking***

Have you ever stopped to consider what your job is? Yes, yes,
I know: your title is vice president (VP) of marketing, human
resources (HR) benefits manager, or chief operating officer. But
going beyond your title, what is the essence of your job? What
aspects of your daily work create real value for your customers?

From the perspective of Lean, there are three kinds of
activities: value-added work, non-value-added (but necessary)
work—also called "incidental" work—and waste. (Some pur-
ists will distinguish between the last two categories as type I
waste and type II waste. But rather than trying to remember
that opaque terminology, I prefer non-value-added work and

waste.) For an activity to be considered value added, it must meet three criteria[1]:

1. The customer must be willing to pay for the activity.
2. The activity must transform the product or service in some way.
3. The activity must be done correctly the first time.

In other words, the starting point for defining value is what your customer has asked you for—whether that customer is a paying client, a colleague, your boss, or even yourself. Value-added work comprises the actions that move your work closer to what that customer needs. Non-value-added work (or "incidental" work) may not move the value forward, but it is essential to your ability to do value-added work. And finally, waste is just that. Waste. To paraphrase Ernest Hemmingway, it's the difference between motion and action.

It's important to note that calling an activity value added or non-value added is not a judgment about the person doing that work. Sometimes, systems or policies force you to do non-value-added work or waste. (I mean, really: Does a florist or a barber really need a special licensing exam? Probably not, but it's necessary to provide that service.)

I should emphasize that it's difficult to see waste and value from your customers' perspective. Think, for example, about ordering a meal at a McDonald's drive-thru window. Is the lag time between ordering and receiving the meal waste? From McDonald's perspective, that's where the value is created—the processing of food. But from the perspective of a customer who decides to use the drive-thru, the value is in speed and convenience (often at the expense of food quality and price). Similarly, are the bathrooms, multiple ordering lanes, and clean interior of the restaurant value added? To eat-in customers, absolutely. But to drive-thru customers, the time, effort, and money invested in these areas are probably waste. The point here is that what's value added from one customer's perspective may be pure waste from a different customer's perspective.[2]

Nevertheless, if you look around you, you'll see legions of entrepreneurs, managers, executives, and others who are confusing activity with value creation. Their days are completely consumed with activities that customers just don't care about and certainly won't want to pay for: HR training. Pointless meetings. Shuffling papers that litter their offices. Scouring their hard drives and e-mail folder trees for important messages. Writing and rewriting to-do lists—while procrastinating on the difficult or unpleasant tasks. Correcting errors that they or their colleagues make. All manner of firefighting and crisis management. Be honest: how much of your day is consumed with these activities?

Figure 1.1 shows some common examples of value-added work, non-value-added work, and waste that you can see if you walked into any office.

This definition of value is actually a pretty high bar to jump over. If you were to track your daily activities, you would probably be shocked at how little time you spend on value-added work—and I'm not talking about the time you spend on Facebook, either. The truth is that the vast majority of your *work-related* activities don't meet these three criteria. And this is where many personal productivity books (in my opinion) go awry: They're totally focused on helping you get work—any work—done, without considering whether that work is value added. They fail to challenge you on the most important question of all: Is this work that you're getting better at doing something *you should even be doing in the first place?* Sure, you can become an e-mail ninja and get your inbox down to zero by the end of each day. But, given that much of the stuff in your inbox is garbage anyway, wouldn't you be better off figuring out how to reduce the volume of incoming mail? Or, perhaps you've reduced the time it takes you to prepare your monthly sales meeting

Job	Value-Added-Activity	Non-Value Added Activity	Waste
Lawyer	Drafting patent claim	Calculating billable hours	Correcting errors made by associates
Shoe designer	Choosing colors and materials	Entering information into product spec sheet	Resending lost files to the factory
Surgeon	Operating on a patient	Filling out billing codes	Waiting to begin a delayed procedure
Architect	Designing a house	Taking continuing education classes	Following up with a materials supplier on delayed samples
Florist	Arranging a flower display	Budgeting for newspaper ad campaign	Replacing a chipped vase
Underwriter	Determining premiums	Studying new rate tables	Looking for lost paper or electronic files

Figure 1.1 Examples of value-added work, non-value-added work, and waste in any office.

PowerPoint presentation from three hours to two ... but do you even need the PowerPoint? Does the sales team? Perhaps a one-page summary report would be faster, easier, and more valuable.

It's astonishingly easy to forget that the work on which you spend so many of your waking hours must be guided by *what* your customers need. In fact, they couldn't care less *how* you get the work done. They don't want inputs (e.g., focus groups, training sessions, PowerPoint reports) or "deliverables." They want outputs and answers. They want results that solve their problems in the shortest time possible for a reasonable fee. Therefore, you should always be mindful not to accelerate activities that look productive but don't actually provide value for your customer.

Most distressingly, the work that generally gets short shrift in these busy days is the value-added work that customers actually care about. George Gonzalez-Rivas and Linus Larsson expressed this situation beautifully:

> We think that the appearance of being busy and overloaded is simply a management proxy for effort and productivity. … But in the absence of meaningful measurements, we settle for the Plato's Cave version of productivity—a cluttered desktop, an overloaded calendar, and workers running from meeting to meeting.[3]

Why Is It So Tough to Create Value?

The way your organization works—and more importantly, for the purposes of this book, the way *you* work—probably hasn't changed much over the years. For example, think about how you share documents with colleagues: I'll bet that you're still e-mailing them back and forth, creating multiple copies of the same document, clogging the mail server, and creating confusion regarding which version really is the final copy of finalbudgetv5.xls, even though there are now excellent alternatives (shared drives, SlideRocket, Google Docs, and Dropbox, just to name a few) to this practice. Or, you're wallpapering your office with to-do items on Post-it® notes that invariably get lost or ignored, rather than using software like reQall or a low-tech kanban (which we'll discuss in another chapter) to keep it safe and organized within the context of your work.

Or, think about the way that bureaucracies create oceans of worthless activity for employees. One organization I know had strict purchasing rules that forbade people from buying anything for themselves; as a result, staff had to fill out extensive paperwork, submit (a paper copy) to the procurement office, and wait for three weeks to get a $50 telephone headset. Hospital nurses, who handle most of the patient paperwork, spend hours per week copying and reentering the same information in different formats on different forms for different departments.

Bob's Story: Getting Rid of Academic Waste

Bob left industry in 1999 and became a university professor. Driven by the desire to improve his productivity and performance as a professor, he quickly started applying Lean principles and practices to the way he designed and delivered his courses. He focused on reducing errors, variation, and rework for himself, and helping students avoid suffering needlessly lower grades due to ambiguity in homework assignments and evaluations.

Bob standardized and searched for abnormalities—deviations from the ideal state—in his work and his colleagues' work. For example, he noticed that some faculty regularly missed appointments with students due to a lack of visual controls. He also noticed that students frequently stood in line outside the professor's office to have the teacher clarify something he didn't explain well in class. This line of waiting students was a clear sign of waste and defects in the "production" of fully educated students.

By rooting out abnormalities in his teaching process and his workplace—the classroom—he has reduced errors in interpretation of his assignments. As a result, he rarely sees students during office hours—they don't need further explanation of the topics he covered in class. His homework assignment questions are narrowly focused, unambiguous, and carefully designed to help students achieve specific learning outcomes.

The result of this focus on value is extremely high student satisfaction. Students often tell Bob that the courses they had with him were the best ones they took in college.

Bob explains, "This rewarding outcome has always been driven by two simple questions: What can I do to improve my teaching in every class and every course? How can I improve students' learning experience so that they will actually apply in the real world what they learned in the classroom?"

I'll leave the discussion of business process improvement for the entire organization to the excellent Lean books already on the market. But it's essential to examine the way you work *within* your organization to discover how to remove some of the waste and non-value-added work that fill your hours.

What the Heck Is Your Work, Anyway?

In any discussion of value, it's essential, first and foremost, to figure out who your customers are and what they want. That's your work.

I want to distinguish here between your "job" and your "work." Your job has some sort of fancy title and incorporates the formal requirements and trappings of your position. By contrast, your work is your real value-creating activities. Your job description probably isn't very helpful in figuring this out. It usually bears only the faintest relation to the job you actually do. (Plus, it's written in turgid HR and business jargon that makes sense to no one except the folks who define job classifications for a living.)

To identify your work, you need to identify the various customers you serve and the various value streams in which you operate. That's the first step in determining what value-added work is for you.

The "customer value" map in Figure 1.2 is a good way to begin seeing your customers and, if relevant, the value they are requesting from you. This is a map from one of my previous jobs. Customers are listed above each line in bold

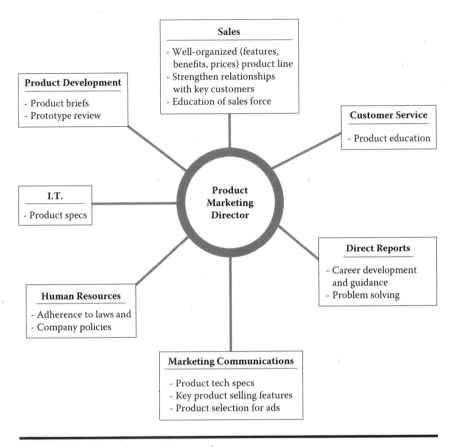

Figure 1.2   Sample customer value map.

letters; the value each customer wants is listed below each line.

You'll notice that by looking at my job on the map in this way, you are better able to focus on *value*, not on specific activities or on "deliverables."

Let me be more specific about that: My direct reports, for example, didn't really want corporate performance evaluations from me. What they really wanted was guidance in developing their careers and improving their skills. The performance evaluation was just a tool (and not a very good one, for that matter) for delivering that value. As another example, the VP of sales worked together with the chief financial officer (CFO) to forecast revenue for the year. He needed pricing, margins, and target volumes from me—but he didn't need me to attend all the finance meetings.

Even if you're an independent contractor or an entrepreneur, this map and the thinking behind it still apply. Obviously, you have a variety of customers who benefit from your services—that's easy. But, your biggest customer, most likely, is yourself: You are the beneficiary of your marketing activities, your bookkeeping, and the classes you take. You could easily make a value stream map that represents business development, financial management, and education as separate streams.

Here's the key point: Focusing on the value to the customer (even when you are the customer) frees you up to improve both *what* you do and *how* you do it. Once you have that perspective, you're unshackled from preconceptions of how to do your job, and you can see more clearly how to create value and reduce waste.

Going to the *Gemba*

> A desk is a dangerous place from which to watch the world.
>
> **—John le Carré**

If you spend any time at all with someone who knows about Lean, you won't be able to finish your first cup of coffee before you hear that person talk about "going to the *gemba*." The *gemba* is a Japanese word that refers to the place where work is actually done. If you're in a factory, the gemba might be a particular production line; it's not the plant manager's office. If you're in company headquarters, the gemba in question might be the accounting department where invoices are processed, and most definitely not the executive conference room.

Lean practitioners are obsessed with going to the gemba because it's only there that you can grasp the reality of a situation and fully understand a problem. For example, it's only by going to the gemba and seeing the customer service reps struggle to navigate through your expensive new software package that you can begin to understand why misshipments and customer returns have spiked. It's because the order entry screens are poorly laid out, and the reps have difficulty entering the data correctly. Without going to the gemba, without seeing people struggle with the software, you might think that your reps are sloppy, lazy, or just don't care. No report from the information technology (IT) department can substitute for the insight that comes from direct observation.

Obviously, the gemba for your work is the place where you actually do your job. You might think, then, that you don't need to go to the gemba. After all, there's nothing there that you have not seen a thousand times already. But, as Yogi Berra is reputed to have said (and with Yogi, you can never be sure what he really said and what's simply apocryphal— even he doesn't know), "You can see a lot just by looking." And the truth is that you probably haven't looked—really looked—at your work honestly and objectively in a long time (or maybe ever).

Take a look at your inbox, for example. How many of the messages that you read and write each day are actually related to what your customers want? How much of your daily activity is truly value-added work (using the three criteria I listed)? Odds are, it's a pretty low percentage. Only you don't see it because you haven't really looked.

As peculiar as it sounds, you have to go to your own gemba. You have to observe what you do and how you do it to spot the value and spot the waste in your work. That's not

Start Time	End Time	Activity	Planned or Unplanned?	Value-Added/ Incidental/Waste
8:30	8:42	Read and write e-mail	P	Incidental
8:42	8:45	Review budget	P	Value-added
8:45	8:46	Read new e-mail re: today's absent employees	U	Waste
8:46	8:50	Review budget	P	Value-added
8:50	9:00	Colleague asks for help with Powerpoint slides	U	Incidental
9:00	9:30	Prepare target specs for new product	P	Value-added
9:30	9:35	Explain to boss why I won't attend 9:30 meeting	U	Waste
		Etc....		

Figure 1.3 Time-tracking log.

easy, of course, because we're all terrible observers of ourselves. But assuming that you don't have piles of money to pay people to watch you work, you can at least log what you do during the day and how long you spend doing it.

I know that the prospect of maintaining a daily activity log for a week or so is probably about as appealing as treating a raging case of scabies, but it is a great way to get a handle on the value-added work, incidental work, and waste in your day. Figure 1.3 is an example of such a log.

What's It All about?

These exercises—the customer value map and the time-tracking log—are simple tools that will help you clarify what you do each day. The prospect of filling these out is probably uninspiring at best, and daunting at worst. But if you're serious about improving the work that you do—about creating more value with less effort—then these are necessary first steps. First, you have to identify your customer and the customer's needs. Then, you have to figure out what activities are necessary to meet those needs. It's as simple as that.

The purpose of this book is to reconnect you with the value-creating portion of your work. As you go through the chapters, you'll learn to see the common (but difficult to spot) waste in your work and how to eliminate it. You'll also learn how to apply the concept of continuous improvement to your work. Ultimately, by learning to identify the value and the waste in your daily activities, you can approach what George Gonzalez-Rivas and Linus Larsson called the Platonic ideal of what your job should be.

Let's get started.

Next Steps

■ Create a customer value map: Identify your downstream customers and the value that they demand from you. Include yourself and your needs in this map. Don't focus on tasks or inputs; focus on what benefit they need. (You may find it useful actually to *ask* them what they want.)
■ Complete a time-tracking log for one week.

Notes

1. *The Hitchhiker's Guide to Lean,* Jamie Flinchbaugh and Andy Carlino, Society of Manufacturing Engineers, Dearborn, MI, 2006, 14.
2. Thanks to Kevin Meyer, founder of the Evolving Excellence blog and the president of Factory Strategies Group, for this outstanding example.
3. *Far from the Factory,* George Gonzalez-Rivas and Linus Larsson, Productivity Press, New York, 2011, 108.

Chapter 2

Spotting Value, Spotting Waste

Allison's Story

Allison is an anesthesiologist at a major hospital in New York. Real estate prices being what they are in the country's most expensive city, her office is only slightly bigger than a closet (that's a broom closet, not a cedar-paneled, walk-in, McMansion-size closet). We're talking a windowless room about 60 square feet, with a desk, computer, and an office chair. And a bookshelf. Oh, and a wall of file cabinets.

Every horizontal surface of Allison's office (except for her chair) is covered—no, buried—in paper: printed out e-mails, regular mail, departmental memos, receipts from the last conference she attended, a decade's worth of professional journals … well, you get the idea. The place is a monument to the paper products industry.

Now, given that Allison does her clinical work in the operating room and doesn't see patients in her office, you might think that the mess is without consequence. After all, it only affects her, not the surgeons or the patients. Moreover, it only interferes with the administrative aspects of her job, not critical patient care issues. But you'd be wrong. Allison's hospital is also a teaching hospital, which means that she's expected to write grants to bring in funds for academic research, and she's supposed to publish her findings.

Want to guess how many papers Allison has published in the past two years? Zero.

She justifies her lack of academic productivity by explaining that her clinical responsibilities are so onerous that she has no time to find available grants and apply for them. To be fair, she does work a long day, and she doesn't get as much academic time as she'd like. But when you watch her for a while, you see that's not the whole story.

It turns out that on days Allison works in her office, she's awfully busy. She spends time moving paper from the left side of the desk to the right side. She spends time looking for articles and printouts. She spends time looking for basic office supplies. She spends time searching for and printing out journal articles that she's already printed out—two or three times before. She even spends time feeling badly about herself, embarrassed by the appearance of her office and struggling to focus on her projects for the day.

Taiichi Ohno, the father of Lean production at Toyota (and by all accounts a real hard-ass) used to draw a chalk circle on the ground in the factory (the infamous "Ohno circle") and make people stand there for hours simply watching production. He believed that unless you really observed the flow of materials and people, you couldn't see or understand the waste in a process. If Ohno were still alive and went to Allison's office, he'd probably throw up because her frantic activity is pretty much nothing *but* waste. Her efforts result in nothing of value for her own professional development, for the reputation of the hospital, or for the progression of medical knowledge.

Allison isn't alone, even if her story is dramatic. A 1997 *Wall Street Journal* survey of 2600 executives revealed that they spend six weeks per year simply *looking* for information. Not doing anything with that information to build their businesses or service their customers—just looking for it. Of course, that survey was conducted before e-mail led to an explosion in corporate communication. Now, even with Google desktop search and other similar engines, the situation isn't any better. The *Wall Street Journal* reported in 2007 that Chevron was investing tens of millions of dollars for an information technology (IT) system upgrade because employees were spending between 1½ to 3 days per month just searching for the information they needed to do their jobs.[1]

It goes on: Studies by the Delphi Group and the Butler Group found that employees spend one-quarter of their time looking for information, and estimated that searching accounted for 10% of labor costs. Independent internal studies at Intel and Cisco found that their employees spend one day per week searching for information.[2]

Ohno is famous for his "7 Wastes"[3] and although he never talked about the waste of "looking for," surely he would see that as one of the causes of unnecessary waiting (which is one of the seven wastes). Certainly, he'd classify the shuffling of piles of paper, and the continual sorting and resorting of e-mail by sender/date/attachment, as wasted motion. In a manufacturing setting with a conveyer belt, the cost of these wastes is generally more obvious (well, obvious to people involved with Lean, anyway): Workers struggle to find the right wrench before the piece moves past them, or people in an assembly area stand around waiting for a part to arrive.

But the cost is no less significant in an office. If you have to put on a pith helmet like Howard Carter searching for King Tut every time you need a document, you're not likely to get a lot done. In Allison's case, the chaos of her office prevents her from focusing on her academic work, allocating time to it, and working efficiently on it. In Chevron's case, the overwhelming bulk of electronic data reduces productivity by as much as 15%, as measured by the number of days each month lost to searching.

Probably the last thing you wanted or expected when you started reading this book was to be hectored about keeping your office neat and tidy, like your mother yelling at you to pick your socks up off the floor. You've got enough going on without some clown doing a white glove test on your desk. However, just as organization and cleanliness on the plant floor is an essential element of a true Lean transformation, it's also an essential element of a Lean transformation in the office. As Ohno once said, "Eliminating waste is not the problem. Identifying it is."

Introducing 5S

Knowledge workers face a daunting task identifying their real work. People working on an assembly line or in an operating room can easily see the work: It's that piece of metal right there on the conveyer belt, or the patient lying there on the table. But for knowledge workers, the job inputs arrive in a variety of formats—e-mails, electronic document attachments, pieces of paper, voice mail, conversations in an office, a hallway, or the break room—and much of it is intangible. Also, the incoming flow of work is "lumpy." There's often no clear rhythm or cadence to the work as it comes in, so you can't even predict when it will arrive. Even worse, sometimes it becomes obsolete even before you've had a chance to address it. Just think of the last time 14 budget revisions crossed your desk in the space of three days.

For all these reasons, knowledge workers struggle to keep value visible. It gets buried in waste. Take a tour of your colleagues' offices; look at the piles of paper on the desk, the hundreds (thousands?) of e-mails stacked up in their e-mail inboxes, the Post-it notes stuck to any clear horizontal or vertical surface, and you've got a clear image of the waste that I'm talking about.

This is where the Lean tool of 5S comes in.

The term *5S* comes from five Japanese words that define an organizational and visual management system. All five words begin with an *s* sound, so someone decided to translate them into English words that begin with *s* as well. I'm not convinced this was the brightest decision ever made—some of the translations are clunky at best and confusing at worst—but the significance of the 5S concept is now universally understood in the Lean world, even if the nuances of each word are sometimes difficult to grasp.

In some respects, 5S is the foundation of Lean. It's not just about "cleaning your room" or being faster at finding your stapler, with all the triviality that implies. In reality, the decisions that 5S forces you to make, and the discipline it imposes, is the basis for much of what we'll talk about in this book. It's the basis for spotting waste, for creating systems that enable work to flow more efficiently, and for helping to clarify "standard work"[4] in the complex, highly variable, office environment. To be sure, applying 5S yields time savings from not having to search for information. But the more significant benefit comes from surfacing abnormalities and waste in processes so they can be fixed.

Some people will claim that 5S isn't really important for knowledge workers unless they're sharing an office space or a desk with someone else. Drawing a parallel to shadow boards for tools, they'll say that an engineer or an art director has never lost a computer mouse or a stapler on his or her desk. Or, they'll think of the inane 5S policies that Kyocera Corporation has in place, which, as the *Wall Street Journal* reported, not only calls for organization in the workplace, but aesthetic uniformity. Sweaters can't hang on the backs of chairs, personal items can't be stowed beneath desks and the only decorations allowed on cabinets are official company plaques or certificates.[5]

But that's not what I'm talking about. 5S for knowledge workers means 5S for the information you manage, not rules about where you can hang your sweater.

What Is Information 5S?

Before going into details for each word, it's helpful to see them laid out in Japanese and English (Table 2.1).

Table 2.1   5S Term Translation

Japanese Term	Translation	Description
Seiri	Sort	Throw out obsolete and useless items. Sort remaining items by frequency of use.
Seiton	Straighten or set in order	Arrange tools in a manner that promotes smooth workflow: a place for everything, and everything in its place.
Seiso	Shine or sweep	Keep the workplace clean, which includes the concept of preventive and corrective maintenance.
Seiketsu	Standardize or systematize	Develop a consistently organized workspace.
Shitsuke	Sustain	Have a system for ongoing support and maintenance of the first four elements.

Figure 2.1   Al Gore's office.

It's easy to picture 5S in a manufacturing setting: clean machines, tape outlines around equipment, shadow boards for tools, a garbage-free floor, and so on. In some respects, 5S for manufacturing is easy because the work at each station is done exactly the same way, every time, by each person. It's easy to define the "right" setup and layout. But what does 5S look like in an office? Desk jockeys do dozens of different types of jobs each day—reading and writing e-mail, preparing spreadsheets, analyzing large budget binders, calling customers. Moreover, each person does it a bit differently; there's no "right" way to prepare a sales presentation. How can you bring 5S to a fundamentally variable environment?

To answer that question, it's best to first define what 5S in the office *is not*. It is not what's depicted in Figure 2.1. Even to someone who isn't a Lean expert, it's pretty clear that global warming activist Al Gore is violating all of the 5S tenets:

■ **Seiri (sort):** There is plenty of useless crap (i.e., old or obsolete information) jumbled in with valuable material.

- **Seiton (set in order):** This layout doesn't support smooth workflow: Where would Al put something to read or edit? How would he reach the stuff on the other side of the desk without getting up, walking around to the front of the desk, and walking back to his chair?
- **Seiso (shine):** Clean? Hah. You can bet that he's not been through most of those piles in weeks, if not months.
- **Seiketsu (standardize):** There's no organizational system to track and find any of the work in progress and valuable reference information. And there is no way for him to tell another person where to find something.
- **Shitsuke (sustain):** There is nothing *to* sustain, unless you're talking about general chaos.

Counter to what you might think, 5S in the office is also *not* what's shown in Figure 2.2. This layout is an example of what Mark Graban, author of *Lean Hospitals*, would call "LAME"— Lean as misguidedly executed.[6] It twists the goal of 5S—to make abnormalities visible and to reduce waste through improved workplace organization and visual management—by

Figure 2.2   Dan's LAME desktop.

using those tools to shackle people to a pointless standard. Yes, this desk layout is neat, tidy, and organized, with a place for everything and everything in its place, but to what end? How does this help the person do his or her job?

Real 5S in an office frees you from the waste of looking for the things you need. Those things are both the tools of your trade—the computer, a stapler, pens, printer paper, and so on—and also the information you're working on, such as a budget, the draft of a speech, or a new purchasing policy. A good 5S system makes it fast and easy to access those things so that you can do the important work you're being paid to do. But that's just the beginning.

Joe's Story: One Ring (Binder) to Rule Them All

Joe works for a medical device manufacturer and often spends his days running from meeting to meeting. He used to carry yellow pads or assorted other pieces of paper to take notes but found that he'd often lose important items—or spend too much time looking for items—that he wanted to track. He developed a single notebook system to solve this problem.

He buys the same notebook over and over from a standard office supply store. (By using the same notebook all the time, it makes a neat set of books on his shelf for reference.) Everything goes into that notebook: every meeting, every phone call, every set of thoughts—all of them go into the notebook. In a very real way, the notebook is a chronological log of everything he does at work.

Each event starts at the top of a new page. He labels the event ("Review with Kevin"; "Acme Vendor meeting"; "Thoughts on Project X"; "Phone with Wayne re: SLRA") and dates it. Then he makes notes. If it takes multiple pages, he notes with an arrow at the bottom of the page that the event continues.

How does he find information later? Easy.

At the top right of each pair of pages, he puts a page number, counting by twos. (As Joe says, "I can do the math. If page 174 is on the right, then the left page must be page 173.") Critically, he has a table of contents on the first page of each notebook where he logs the page number of every significant event in that notebook. The chronology

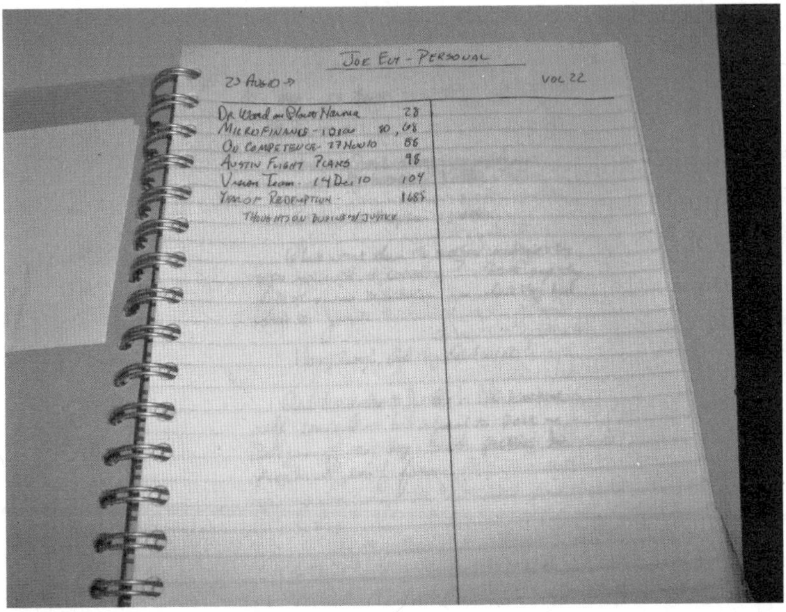

Figure 2.3 Joe's notebook.

keeps everything in order, enabling him to find what he needs quickly and easily (Figure 2.3).

He numbers the volumes consecutively on the cover and adds the dates spanned in that notebook on the cover. He uses a small Post-it tag to mark the next blank page so that he can easily open to that spot. The result is that he only needs one notebook—for everything.

A Lesson from the Chefs

If you've never been to a restaurant kitchen, you'd be amazed at the contrast with the "front of the house" where you dine. It's crazy back there, particularly during the lunch and dinner rushes. People are shouting and cursing; waiters, cooks, and "runners" are rushing through the kitchen trying to get orders out the door—it's barely controlled chaos.

This is true except for one spot: the chef's "mise-en-place," the area where the chef organizes and arranges the ingredients he or she will be using that night. Chef and author Anthony Bourdain explained the importance of mise-en-place in *Kitchen Confidential*:

> Mise-en-place is the religion of all good line cooks. Do not f**k with a line cook's "meez"—meaning their set-up, their carefully arranged supplies of sea salt, rough-cracked pepper, softened butter, cooking oil, wine, back-ups and so on. As a cook, your station, and its condition, its state of readiness, is an extension of your nervous system—and it is profoundly upsetting if another cook or, God forbid, a waiter—disturbs your precisely and carefully laid-out system. The universe is in order when your station is set up the way you like it: you know where to find everything with your eyes closed, everything you need during the course of the shift is at the ready at arm's reach, your defenses are deployed. If you let your mise-en-place run down, get dirty and disorganized, you'll quickly find yourself spinning in place and calling for back-up. I worked with a chef who used to step behind the line to a dirty cook's station in the middle of the rush to explain why the offending cook was falling behind. He'd press his palm down on the cutting board, which was littered with peppercorns, spattered sauce, bits of parsley, breadcrumbs and the usual flotsam and jetsam that accumulates quickly on a station if not constantly wiped away with a moist side-towel. "You see this" he'd inquire, raising his palm so that the cook could see the bits of dirt and scraps sticking to his chef's palm, "That's what the inside of your head looks like now. *Work clean!*"[7]

Want to know what 5S is, without resorting to all those difficult-to-pronounce Japanese words? It is mise-en-place. (Of course, we've just substituted French for Japanese, so there may not be any advantage for you.) It is your physical workspace and your information precisely laid out so that you can find anything with your eyes closed. It's the clean, well-ordered inside of your head so that you can stay on top of all the work your boss, colleagues, and customers are dumping on you. Poor Allison's head, of course, is littered with the anesthesiologist's version of peppercorns, spattered sauce, bits of parsley, and breadcrumbs. But quite frankly, if a line cook during the dinner rush can keep his or her workspace organized, so can you.

Applying 5S to Information

Seiri (sort) means making decisions about each individual piece of information that has accumulated over time—e-mails, files, reports, journals, presentations, links to Web sites, and so on. Whether you choose actually to use it for a project this week, move it to a file for future reference, or toss it, the simple act of deciding what to do with each item can reveal systemic (or personal) problems by forcing you to assess how you work. For example, the presence of handwritten phone lists at your desk is a good indication that the online phone directory is clunky and hard to use. Or, if you're a medical assistant, a sloppy pile of patient charts on your desk might indicate that there's something wrong with the system of retrieving, reviewing, signing, and filing essential patient information. (You can also be sure that whatever is wrong with the system will lead to lost charts, missing information, and wasted time in looking for it.) Notice, though, that neither the phone lists nor the charts would be clearly visible without cleaning up the information flotsam and jetsam that wash up on your desk.

Seiton (set in order) ensures that critical information can be found quickly and easily. This is the wisdom behind a surgeon's instrument tray being laid out precisely the same way every time, the military teaching recruits how to pack their rucksacks, and a chef's mise-en-place being set up and ready: When there's an emergency (or at 8 p.m. on a Saturday night with every table full), the surgeon, the soldier, and the chef can't afford the time to hunt for something in a panic. But, even if you don't work in an operating room or run a restaurant kitchen, what happens when you, or your boss, goes on vacation? If activity slows or grinds to a halt because the necessary information can't be found, there's a real problem with the system: Daily work should flow in your absence as smoothly as if you were there.

The concept of preventive maintenance embedded within seiso (shine) is another aspect of 5S that elevates it above simple desktop or office organization. Regular attention to the information coming into your office ensures that you'll know if projects are in danger of falling behind schedule or whether invoices are at risk of not being paid on time—and enables you to act before the situation becomes critical. Seiton and seiso also tie into the notion of visual management that is so important to Lean: the ability to see, quickly and easily, any abnormalities in the status of a process. (We'll talk more about visual management in a further chapter.)

Seiketsu (standardize) demands the development of a precise routine for the most easily controlled element in a chaotic environment: cleaning and organizing a workspace. At first blush, this may seem unnecessarily anal—I mean, do you *really* need a system for cleaning out your e-mail inbox and processing the papers that piled up during your vacation? Nevertheless, there's wisdom in the concept. Having a system for processing and cleaning up all the information in your office means that you'll get through the activity faster and with a lower risk of missing something important. The deeper value of developing a system for a task like 5S, however, is that it acts as a springboard for the development of standard work for other areas of your job.

Now, let us imagine how 5S could have helped Allison. By sorting and setting in order the papers she had accumulated over time, she'd have better visibility into both the information she already had for her research in her office, and the information she still needed to acquire. "Shining" her work would have given her a regular status update on her research paper, which would have helped define a plan for her to get the work done. Finally, standardizing her 5S activities would have helped her develop the discipline to do her academic research more frequently, instead of allowing it to sink, literally and metaphorically, below the piles of trash in her office, or get pushed aside by other competing commitments. To be sure, the rigor of 5S isn't a panacea for all her problems or a guarantee that Allison would have published three papers in the past year—but it certainly would have helped by making the work necessary for getting published clearer and more apparent.

The $14 Million Check

In 2007, an employee in the risk department at a large investment bank was promoted to vice president. He was put on the fast track for high-potential employees because he showed so much promise. A few weeks after his promotion, his boss, one of the managing directors, stopped by to see how he was doing. She was surprised at how messy his office was: stacks of paper on his desk, with more piles on the floor. Half-joking, she told him that if he wanted to continue moving up the ranks, he'd really have to learn how to organize—messiness just didn't look good in the eyes of the top brass.

A crumpled piece of paper in one of the stacks caught her eye. Idly, she removed it, smoothed it out, and was shocked to see it was a refund check from the Internal Revenue Service (IRS) for $14 million—dated six months earlier. With the U.S. federal debt now exceeding $14 trillion, it's hard to remember a time when $14 million—and the interest on it—was real money, but in fact it was.

As you'd guess, the managing director was apoplectic. She demanded to know why the check was still sitting on his desk instead of having been turned over to the appropriate department. The employee complained that with all the special projects he was working on and all the deliverables with short timelines that were weighing on him, he just didn't have a chance to deal with it. He had *meant* to, of course, but he just didn't have the time, and then, frankly, he forgot about it as it disappeared into the pile. Besides, he wasn't even sure to whom he was supposed to send it for processing.

The story didn't end well for our high-potential employee. Combined with another $8 million check that went missing (not malfeasance, just more sloppiness), he was fired by the end of the day.

The obvious connection to 5S is that an uncluttered desk, combined with regular and systematic maintenance of his workspace, would have avoided this whole fiasco and enabled our high-potential employee to keep his job. And that's true. But as mentioned before, one of the main benefits of 5S is the surfacing of abnormalities—and this story illustrates at least two beauties. For starters, it's clear that the investment bank lacked a process for tracking refund checks. The IRS sent the bank $22 million, but it took a random visit to someone's office and an idle poke at a pile actually to find that those checks existed. Even if you don't know anything about how an investment bank works, it's hard not to consider that an abnormality.

In addition, there is an abnormality in human resources (HR) training and development: Someone promoted to vice president wasn't taught how to handle IRS refund checks. Even if there is no hard-and-fast system at the bank, surely there must be some ad hoc or unofficial method for dealing with them. 5S, rigorously applied, would have identified that problem within the week of the arrival of the check, long before the managing director's arrival in the vice president's office.

So, what does office 5S look like? Rather than shoehorn my recommendations into each of the 5Ss, I think it's better to paint a picture of the 5S workspace. That way you won't get bogged down into worrying whether something is "sort" or "straighten."

The Desktop

First, it's important to realize that the desktop is a workspace. It's not a storage space.

That is to say, the desktop is a place for you to think, to analyze, to solve problems, and to create customer value. It is not a place for you to pile up papers that you have not yet had a chance to read or put away. It's not a place for 27 pens and 9 highlighters (of which only 3 actually work), nor is it an office supply closet. It's not a repository for napkins, chopsticks, and enough soy sauce packets to float the Queen Mary. It's a place for you as a professional and your tools.

A surgeon's workspace is the operating room and operating table. Your workspace is your (considerably more prosaic) cubicle and desk. Just as a surgeon only keeps what he or she needs at hand, you should only keep what you need on the top of your desk. So, you'll want to have your computer, phone, pens, and so on—your tools—on your desktop. But, you don't need piles of old paper and dozens of professional journals you've been planning to read since the Nixon Administration.

This approach to the desktop supports the concept of one-piece flow. In a Lean system, there's only one thing in front of the operator at any time—whatever it is that the downstream customer requires. Whether it's a rearview mirror assembly for a car or the latest budget revision, the person does not pile up inventory or work in process. In the same way, there should only be one thing—an invoice, a design for next season's shoe model, the abstracts being referred to for a new article—on your desk at any one time. (We'll talk in another chapter about how the calendar can work as a *kanban*—a signal—to show the need to pull more work and begin dealing with that item.)

To manage all the incoming paper, you'll want to have two (or three) stacking trays (Figure 2.4). If you manage them properly, your coworkers won't find it necessary to leave things for you on your chair, your computer keyboard, or taped to your monitor. You'll have one place—and only one—to look for new incoming information. (Paper-based information, that is; e-mail is discussed in its own section.) And that means you'll be faster in finding and processing it. If you think of your inbox like your mailbox at home, this setup makes perfect sense. After all, you'd go crazy if your mailperson left some of your mail in your mailbox, some on your doorstep, and some out on the back porch. You want one place to receive it all.

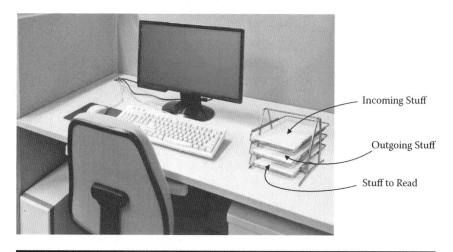

Figure 2.4   Desktop arrangement.

So, the first tray is the inbox. This tray is the home for new stuff you haven't yet had a chance to review—period. It isn't a place for you to put *back* something you've read but don't have the time to handle right now. Once you have picked it up, you can't put it back in the inbox.

Processing your inbox is a piece of work in and of itself. Like it or not, it takes time to go through that pile of paper (or e-mail), and you have to allow for it. Aimlessly sifting through the contents is the first step on the road to organizational hell.

Disrespecting your inbox leads frighteningly quickly to chaos—and waste. With stuff scattered about your workspace, your computer, your phone, your car, and the pockets of your clothes, you'll find yourself engaged in frantic searches for critical information through the blizzard of Post-its stuck to the edges of your computer monitor and the notes buried under piles on your desk. You'll waste time scrolling up and down your e-mail inbox trying to find the one message with a needed phone number. You'll ask someone to resend you information (for the third time) that you just can't find. Or, you'll just ... forget about it entirely. And all the while, the ghost of Taiichi Ohno is shaking his head at the colossal waste of it all.

The second tray is the outbox. This tray holds anything that you need to send out—signed papers, reviewed documents, letters, CDs, and so on. By keeping it in a clearly segregated place, you ensure that these items don't get lost in a pile of documents that you might be working on. The outbox makes it easy for your assistant to pick up these outgoing items, or for you to distribute them on your next trip to the coffee machine.

The third tray holds all your professional reading material—magazines, journals, newsletters, and so on. (It doesn't hold material that you have to read as part of your daily job, such as internal reports.) Now, I know you're looking at the giant stack of journals in your office and thinking, "There's no way I could fit all that into a single tray." However, if you're like most people, only about 10–20% of any journal is interesting or relevant to you. So try this: When a magazine arrives, look at the table of contents, rip out any articles that seem interesting and throw out the rest of the magazine. You'll find that your massive pile of reading has shrunk to something pretty manageable.

The Absurdity of "Out of Sight, Out of Mind"

If you're like most people, you hesitate to put your incoming documents and current projects away in a drawer or file cabinet because you believe fervently that the old chestnut "out of sight, out of mind" is correct. You're convinced that if you clean off your desk and put work away, you'll forget to do it, until finally you are embarrassed at a meeting with your boss, a customer, or the Joint Commission.

The anxiety related to "out of sight, out of mind" is absurd on so many levels it's hard to know where to start debunking it.

1. If seeing the item on your desk actually helped you get it done, it probably wouldn't still be sitting there four months after you carefully put it on the side of your desk … then moved it to the shelf above your desk … and then to the credenza behind you.
2. If seeing the item is critical to taking care of it, then how does it help you to have it buried underneath two and a half inches of paper that came in at a later date? If it's buried in a pile and you cannot see it anymore, then by your own argument you'll forget about it (because you can't really see it anymore). Moreover, if it is buried in a pile of paper and you don't know it's there anymore, then in a

philosophical sense it doesn't really exist; it might as well be a blank piece of paper for all the good it's doing you.

3. If seeing the item on your desk is necessary, then how do you hope to handle any of the work that arrives electronically? You can't "see" it in on your desk in the same way, which by your own logic, dooms you to lose track of it.

4. Keeping something in sight all the time does nothing but ensure that it eventually becomes invisible to you. Our five senses are wonderfully designed to become desensitized to the same repetitive stimulus. That's why people who live near train tracks stop hearing the train when they sleep, why people stop smelling perfume (or garlic, or horse manure) after a few minutes in a room with that odor, and why you stop seeing (I mean, *really* seeing) the piles of paper on your desk. Don't believe me? Take a look at the collection of Post-it notes littering your desk and see if there is a phone number (or two) that you were supposed to do something with, but now you don't recognize them anymore.

Productivity expert David Allen said, "If it's on your mind, it's probably not getting done." When you leave work on your desk in the hopes of reminding yourself to do it, you're trying to keep it on your mind—because you're not doing it. It's far better to put the work away and create a kanban system to ensure that you pull the work at the appropriate time. We'll discuss how this operates in the chapter on flow. For now, suffice it to say that you should keep your desk clean so that you have the physical—and mental—space in which to work.

So, where do you put all this stuff that you're no longer leaving on your desk? Put it into a simple, flexible filing system organized on the principle of frequency of use.

Frequency-Based Organization

The main reason that paper and documents metastasize in the office is that most people's filing systems are inadequate to manage the different types of information that flow through them. The systems never get much more sophisticated than "one of these things is not like the other." For example, people sort all contracts, purchase orders, and invoices by client—one giant file for the Henderson account and another giant file for the Sanchez account. They do the same for the various meetings and committees they attend, for personnel records, and for special projects they manage.

Intuitively, this makes sense. You wouldn't want the Henderson invoice to get lost inside the Sanchez file. But it's not sufficient to manage the huge volume of information that people handle. And, it's only getting worse: Between 1995 and 2000, the consumption of office paper rose almost 15% in the United States.[8] Other research showed that use of the Internet and e-mail can actually cause a rise in paper consumption of up to 40%.[9] Faced with this staggering amount of paper, most systems collapse under the weight of their own engorged manila folders. As a result, the documents that people work with most often at any given time—the high-value documents—are buried in an undifferentiated mass with all the other, low-value documents.

The solution to this problem is separating (seiri/sort) the information you're keeping by the frequency with which you use it. You can do that by creating three groups of files: working, reference, and archive files.

John Wooden's Shoelaces

Before we go further, I want to reassure you that the purpose of creating this system is not to turn you into a file clerk. Lord knows, you've got enough to do already without having to construct your personal version of the Dewey decimal system. No, the purpose of this system is twofold. First, and most obviously, it's designed to eliminate the time you waste looking for information. Second, it allows you to invest your mental energy into something really important, like solving customer problems.

A story about John Wooden is illustrative here.

John Wooden is unquestionably the greatest college basketball coach of all time. His teams at the University of California Los Angeles (UCLA) won 10 national championships in 12 years, including 7 in a row. At one point, they won 88 straight games—that's three and a half undefeated seasons. To put his achievements in perspective, the next coach on the list has four national titles, and none has won more than two consecutive championships.

As he built this basketball powerhouse, he had his pick of the top high school players from around the country. Regardless of who came to play for him, the very first lesson on the first day of practice was always the same: how to put on socks and tie shoelaces. Sounds crazy, right? You'd think that college students wouldn't need to be taught how to do this, especially those who had made it onto the UCLA team. But in Wooden's eyes, this preposterously simple lesson was the foundation for *everything* else he taught: A player couldn't possibly execute complex plays in a game if his shoelaces came untied, or if he was focusing on a blister forming under a poor-fitting sock. The defensive schemes and offensive plays were important, of course, but they had to rest on a rock-solid foundation of properly worn shoes.

Your performance at work is no different. You must have a rock-solid organizational foundation—a 5S foundation—to be able to focus on the complex problems you and your company face each day. You don't want to think about *where* something is; you want to think about *what* you are going to do with it. I'll go even further: You don't want to think *about* your work, you want to *do* your work.

Working Files

Now, back to your piles of paper. The first category you want to create is working files. If you believe (as I do) that most of life adheres to the Pareto principle[10] (the 80–20 rule), 80% of your work will be contained in these files—but these files will only comprise 20% of the paper that's piled up in your office.

Working files meet one of the following criteria: (1) They're used frequently, usually one or more times per week; or (2) they have predictable retrieval. Examples of working files are current client invoices, action items from the last committee meeting, notes to discuss with a direct report in your next one-on-one session, open purchase orders, or a preliminary budget you're developing (Figure 2.5).

Figure 2.5   Working and reference files.

Because we've separated out this 20% of high-value, frequently used, information from the other 80% of the paper, you'll be able to store it at your fingertips for easy access—the file drawer in your desk is a good choice, or some other place nearby.

Your calendar will provide the signal when it is time to "pull" documents from the working files and move them to the desktop (or open and begin working on computer files).

Reference Files

Reference files comprise the other 80% of the papers in your office which you only use 20% of the time. Reference files meet one of the following criteria: (1) They're used infrequently, usually less than once per month; or (2) they have unpredictable retrieval. This folder will hold documents like market research reports, templates and forms, old client information, the company travel expense policy, last year's performance reviews, meeting notes and agendas from last month, and so on. These files are kept in separate drawers or a filing cabinet away from your desk. The information you keep in reference files is not garbage; it's just that you don't use it on a regular basis, so there's no point in keeping it nearby.

Reference files will often mirror your working files. So, you might have a Henderson file in working that contains the current invoices, and you'll have a Henderson file in reference that contains old invoices, correspondence, and charge-backs.

There's an organic flow of information between these categories. When Henderson pays his invoices, they're moved into the reference file. If you need that information a few months later for a dispute over payment, then they're moved back into the Henderson working file. And when the dispute is resolved, they're returned to reference.

Pack rats of the world take note: I'm not asking you to part with that precious phone list from 1988 that you have been diligently saving "just in case" (although you really should). Just dump it in your reference files. If you need it (and deep down, you know you won't), you'll know where it is. In the meantime, you won't have to look at it every time you're retrieving something really important like, say, the Department of Homeland Security Request for Proposal (RFP) you are working on.

The cardinal rule: Don't commingle working and reference items. Commingling this information is what leads to the giant piles on most people's desks and the waste of "looking for."

Archive Files

Even though my 80–20 approach to paper management has mathematically covered it all, there's one more category that will help you apply 5S to the information that flows through you. This is the archive category. Archive files are files that you never plan on using again, but you must keep for legal or policy reasons. Tax returns, files on ex-employees, and (possibly) lyrics from the company's 1996 Christmas party are good examples of archive items. These files should be kept in another drawer in the file cabinet, in a central storage location in the office, or even at an off-site location. They're accessible to you when you need them, but they're out of your way for the 99.44% of the time that you don't. As with the reference files, if you do need these files for some reason, like an IRS audit, it's a simple task to move them into the working file drawer.

The beauty of this structure is that the high-value files— that is, the stuff you use regularly—are kept in the relatively small working drawer. The bulk of files will be in your reference or archive areas, so you don't have to look at them or sift through them to find the high-value information.

Table 2.2

File Type	Expected Retrieval Frequency
Working	Predictable or frequent (one or more times per week)
Reference	Unpredictable or infrequent (less than once per week)
Archive	Never

Table 2.2 summarizes the different characteristics of these file types.

But First ...

The only way to make this work is first to toss all the garbage that has accumulated over the months (years?) that you've been in your office. That's the first step. The Lean gurus define this purging process as "sorting"—as in, sorting the garbage from the value. I prefer to think of it as common sense. There's no point in paying rent on the square footage occupied by cabinets jammed with files inherited from your predecessor three years ago—files you've never looked at. There's no point in creating files for all that useless paper. That would be tantamount to alphabetizing your garbage, and that's pure waste. So, get a dumpster and toss all the detritus that has accumulated over the years—really. If you need it again (and that's unlikely), Google can probably find it for you.

Translating the Concept to Electronics

Although electronic file storage space is nearly limitless and dirt cheap (and getting cheaper by the year), waste of any sort is anathema to the Lean thinker. Just because you *can* store two terabytes of PowerPoint presentations, budget revisions, and cute kitten pictures doesn't mean that you *should*. Fortunately, the working/reference/archive model translates beautifully to your computer storage as well.

In the screenshot in Figure 2.6, you can see how I've created distinct categories for working, reference, and archive information. You can also see how there are two "client" folders—one in working and one in reference. At the time I took this screenshot, the clients listed in the working folder (whose names I oh-so-cleverly disguised) were the ones I was actively engaged with. The ones in the reference folder are the clients that were, for whatever reason, on the back burner or dormant.

You will notice that the computer folders are called "1 Working," "2 Reference," and "3 Archive." The numbers force the computer to do a number sort, rather than an alpha sort, on the folders. Without the numbers, the folders will be sorted with your least-frequently used category (archive) at the top, and the most important (working) at the bottom. Unless you are used to reading Chinese, this doesn't make sense since we read a page from the top left corner downward.

In an age of Google desktop search, though, it's worth asking whether it makes sense to 5S electronic files. After all, if Google can find anything in 0.03 seconds, why spend the time deleting and filing electronic documents? Why spend your time organizing like a librarian, when you can dig like an archeologist when you need to? That's a fair question.

But first, your organization may not allow you to install something like Google desktop. For example, complying with the Health Insurance Portability and Accountability Act of 1996 (HIPAA) keeps many hospitals from allowing employees to install these types of programs. Second, there's value in reducing the number of false positives (irrelevant results) you'll get if you store everything in a giant file and rely on Google

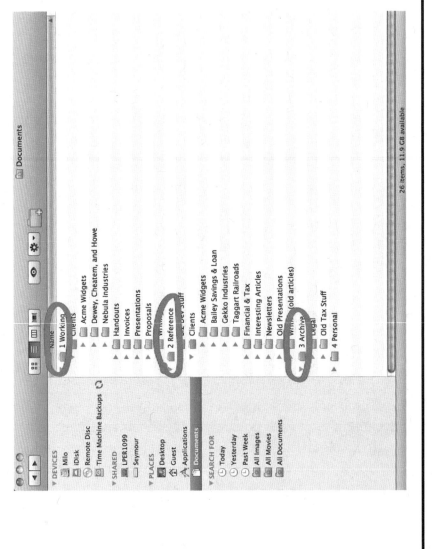

Figure 2.6 File folder tree screenshot.

desktop search. Last, there is something to be said for consistency in behavior: If you're going to be slovenly about managing your electronic information, it's more likely that you'll end up being slovenly about physical information and tools.

E-mail: The Problem Child

Bringing 5S to e-mail is more complicated. The working/reference/archive structure doesn't apply well to mail for a variety of reasons.

First, the volume of mail is exponentially larger than any other electronic or physical data you deal with—and much, if not most, of that mail is low value at best and garbage at worst. Second, most people have a desire (and sometimes a legitimate business need) to have the ability to retrieve everything they've ever received going back to the Paleozoic era. Third, because people write so badly, it's usually difficult to sort and categorize the messages you receive. Fourth, the organizational challenge is complicated by the fact that every company has different e-mail retention policies: In some places, you're given large mailbox limits; in others, your information gets archived after a set period; in still other organizations, old mail gets deleted. And, we've not even talked yet about e-mail attachments.

What to do?

I believe that a simple approach is best. Creating an elegant, taxonomically exhaustive folder tree with seven layers of nested folders is the road to madness. You'll spend more time fiddling with mail—filing it, occasionally misplacing it, and trying to find it again—than you can possibly justify. Unless you have a pathological (and dysfunctional) need to be organized on the scale of Phil Hartman's "Anal Retentive Chef" character[11] from *Saturday Night Live*, less is definitely more.

It's helpful to make friends with your delete key. There's really no reason to hold on to the messages about which restaurant you were going to have lunch at on August 19, 2004. If the message clearly has limited utility ("There's leftover birthday cake in the break room"; "Let's meet at 2:30 instead of 3:00"), delete it once it's become obsolete.

For mail that's important to save, create one folder for "processed mail." That's it. This folder acts as the analog to your reference and archive folders. If you don't need to do anything with the mail, when you're done reading it, put it in this folder. Search the folder when you need to—which won't be nearly as often as you think. If you're in the middle of a project that's generating a lot of correspondence that you need to refer back to frequently, create and save a search folder[12] for that project, but keep the mail in the processed mail folder.

But, what about messages that you need to act on in some way? Where should you put the e-mail equivalent of working files? We'll deal with those in the next chapter. For right now, just leave them in your inbox.

Back to Allison

How does all this 5S business tie back to Allison? She embarked on a rigorous 5S program, throwing out the stuff that she didn't need and organizing the paper and electronic files according to frequency of use. This simple change provided her with the ability actually to see what needed her attention and to stay focused on it. (This aspect of visual management is discussed further in a later chapter.) As a result, she reduced the cognitive distractions that kept her from really focusing on her writing. She now regularly spends two to three hours per week on her research and is hoping to publish a paper before the end of the year.

Systemic Information 5S

As I mentioned, 5S applies to both physical and electronic information, and so far I've been talking about using it for personal information management. But applying it to the information flows within an organization is perhaps an even more powerful use of the tool. Think of the reports that you either produce or read: How many of them show similar, or even identical, information? How many of those reports do you really need? I know of one IT department that produced over 350 reports per month for the managers and executives of the company. As part of a 5S initiative, they analyzed all the reports, spoke to their customers (i.e., the managers and executives), and managers and eliminated the obsolete reports, the redundant reports, and the non-user-friendly reports. They reduced the volume to 37.

Similarly, a nursing team at Covenant Health System in Lubbock, Texas, used 5S like a chainsaw to reduce the paperwork burden that threatened to crush them daily. Before they deployed 5S, nurses spent an average of 6.1 hours per 12-hour shift on documentation. Collectively, they handled over 2.2 million forms each year. Even worse, documentation errors often weren't detected for three to five weeks after patient dismissal. A comprehensive 5S initiative involved simplifying, combining, and standardizing forms, leading to a 40% reduction in paperwork and a 48% reduction in time spent filling out documentation.[13] Each nurse recaptured three hours per shift to spend with patients—the activity that they not only love, but which also creates the real value for the patients/customers.

In these two examples, the 5S principles of seiri (sort) and seiton (set in order) were used to reduce systemic waste—of time, effort, and energy—and helped workers spend more time doing something important for customers. This broader application of 5S to the management of information is just as important in reducing waste as the individual application, but has greater impact on both individual and group productivity.

Remember, It's a Means to an End

Let us be honest: There is something about 5S and organization in general that feels trivial at best and remedial at worst, but that's only because you're thinking about the process, not the objective. What you're really trying to do here is make it easier to spot abnormalities and waste, allowing you to focus on creating value for your customers.

From this perspective, you can view 5S as a fundamental building block rather than remediation. It's the foundation of the cathedral of value that you're erecting. In the next chapter, we learn why and how we want to make that value visible.

Next Steps

In keeping with 5S principles, let's apply it to the information in this chapter. Here are your next steps:

- Throw out the crap in your office. Be ruthless. If you haven't looked at a document in two years and have no plan to do so in the future, toss it.
- Buy three stacking trays.
- Buy paper filing supplies: one-third cut manila folders, hanging folders, tabs.
- Make "Inbox," "Outbox," and "Reading" trays and use them for all new incoming papers and files.
- Put all desktop papers into the inbox.
- Create working, reference, and archive file drawers. Folders inside the working file drawer should correspond

to the value streams you identified in your customer value map (Chapter 1).

■ Create working, reference, and archive electronic folders. Folders inside the working folder should correspond to the value streams you identified in your customer value map (Chapter 1).

■ Create a "Processed Mail" e-mail folder and move into it all messages older than 2 weeks. (Don't worry about deleting worthless old messages at this point. You've got so many of them that it's not worth your time.)

■ Make a recurring "5S Maintenance" appointment in your calendar: 30 minutes, once per month.

Notes

1. "Cutting Files Down to Size," Pui-Wing Tam, *The Wall Street Journal*, May 8, 2007.
2. "Socialtext Enterprise Microblogging White Paper," Ross Mayfield, updated September 2009, http://www.socialtext.com/offers/images/Microblogging_whitepaper.pdf.
3. Although Ohno didn't state explicitly that these are the only wastes to be eliminated, most people consider them to be the "classic" wastes to be avoided: (1) overproduction; (2) waiting; (3) transporting; (4) overprocessing; (5) unnecessary inventory; (6) unnecessary motion; (7) defects. Many people add an eighth waste: unused employee creativity.
4. Standard work is the safest, highest-quality, and most efficient way known to perform a particular process or task.
5. "Neatness Counts at Kyocera and at Others in the 5S Club," Julie Jargon, *The Wall Street Journal*, October 27, 2008.
6. http://www.LeanBlog.org/LAME, Mark Graban, "Lean or Lame?," March 27, 2007.
7. *Kitchen Confidential*, Anthony Bourdain, Bloomsbury USA, New York, 2000, 58–59.
8. "The Social Life of Paper," Malcolm Gladwell, *The New Yorker*, March 25, 2002.

9. *The Myth of the Paperless Office*, Abigail J. Sellen and Richard H. R. Harper, MIT Press, Cambridge, MA, 2001.

10. The Pareto principle is named after the Italian economist Vilfredo Pareto, who in 1906 observed that 80% of the land in Italy was owned by 20% of the population.

11. Watch the video of the late Phil Hartman's performance here: http://www.hulu.com/watch/4101/ saturday-night-live-cooking-with-the-anal-rententive-chef.

12. Microsoft's Web site has useful information on search folders in Outlook, including a short tutorial on creating them: http:// office.microsoft.com/en-us/outlook-help/about-search-folders-HP007328474.aspx. Other e-mail clients have their own versions of search folders (in Apple Mail, they're called "smart folders," for example), but the principles are the same. It's well worth learning how to use them.

13. All data are from the presentation, "Breakthroughs in Reducing Nurse Documentation Time," at the Institute for Healthcare Improvement's 22nd Annual National Forum on Quality Improvement in Health Care, December 7, 2010.

Chapter 3

Flow

All we are doing is looking at the time line, from the moment the customer gives us an order to the point when we collect the cash. And we are reducing the time line by reducing the non-value adding wastes.

—Taiichi Ohno

Consider some of these typical wastes in a service environment:

- The time wasted in trying to get back to work after an interruption. That's the time you spend rereading the previous two pages of a document to get back to where you were ... before your coworker asked you for advice. It's the time you spend retracing the formulas you were debugging in a spreadsheet model ... until you replied to an e-mail. It's the time you spend staring at the ceiling trying to remember the paragraph you were writing ... and then you answered the phone.
- The time and effort wasted in picking up "dropped balls." Do you ever forget to do something for a coworker or a customer (or, for that matter, a spouse)? It's waste when

others have to remind you of a commitment you've
made—a waste of waiting for you to get your job done,
a waste of effort in following up with you for the third or
fourth time. And by the way, that's just the waste if they're
successful in reminding you in time; there's even more
waste from product defects, rework, preventable patient
illnesses, and so on if you don't get the work done.

■ The time wasted and defects caused by multitasking.
We mistakenly believe that we're more efficient when
we multitask—in fact, you probably pride yourself on
your ability to multitask. Yet, the research is conclusive:
Multitasking doesn't work. Trying to do two (or more)
things at once slows us down and increases the likelihood of errors.[1]

■ Penalties and fees imposed for work that is turned in late.

■ The time, effort, and energy expended on rework.

■ The erosion of trust among colleagues and irritated
customers.

These are just a few of the common, but less-obvious,
examples of the waste created by a lack of "flow" in your
work. Most companies haven't yet bothered to quantify this
waste because "that's just the way people [or the system]
works." But that way of thinking isn't good enough anymore.
The world is too competitive, and the risks of working the
same way as always are too high. We must bring the same
rigor that we bring to improving assembly-line work and business processes to individual knowledge work.

Flow

In the classic book *Lean Thinking*, authors Dan Jones and Jim
Womack explained how traditional work processes are done
in "batch-and-queue" fashion. Work is sent from department to

department, or from function to function, where it waits to be processed in a large batch. For example, a stamping machine makes all the front fenders in one batch, and then it switches to making all the rear fenders at one time. In an office, you might see a pile of purchase orders sitting in someone's inbox waiting to be processed in a large batch.

The opposite of batch and queue is flow. In a system that flows, work is done on a product continuously, from start to finish, with each step making just what is needed by the next step in the process. The benefit of flow is that tasks can almost always be accomplished more efficiently and accurately when the product is worked on continuously. Flow eliminates non-value-adding steps in the process and aligns activity around value for the customer. It connects the producer with the customer and the customer's needs more closely by avoiding the buildup of piles of inventory through overproduction. It removes obstacles and muddiness in the process and thus delivers higher-quality work faster, with lower costs, less stress, and less effort.

Can we apply this idea to knowledge work?

Absolutely.

Not in exactly the same way as you would in a manufacturing setting—managers and supervisors work in too many value streams, with different types of tasks of differing complexities and multiple time lines—but the same principles apply. You *can* create a process that will raise the quality and efficiency of your work by removing the barriers and impediments to creating value. And thinking about the flow of your work is the key. But, if you want your processes to flow, you have to rethink work practices to eliminate backflows, errors, and stoppages of all sorts so that the production of your products and services can proceed continuously.

If you were to think of all the work that comes to you and emanates from you as a river, you wouldn't see a perfectly channeled, smoothly flowing stream. You'd see a variety of streams and eddies, nearly stagnant in some places and a frothy, turbulent mess in others. You'd have the postsales meeting lull and the late-night chaos spent finalizing the copy and artwork before a client presentation the next day. You would find long-term projects that you've been procrastinating on for two months and work that your boss drops on you at the last minute. There would be no consistency, no flow.

Lack of flow is bad—think stagnant water and West Nile virus. Stagnant water is a breeding ground for mosquitoes that can carry West Nile. Indeed, one of the best ways to prevent the virus from reproducing is to remove standing water—by keeping the water flowing.

Lack of flow is also stressful. Playing beat the clock with the final specs on the latest version of your online vintage Beanie Baby database is an invitation to sleepless nights and health problems. More important, it creates waste. Taiichi Ohno, one of the fathers of the Toyota production system (yes, back to him again), identified seven kinds of waste[2]:

- Correction or defects (e.g., errors in documents)
- Conveyance (e.g., handoffs, movement of documents— even electronically)
- Overproduction (e.g., doing work not requested, extra features)
- Waiting (e.g., waiting for the next step)
- Processing (e.g., extra steps, approvals, and sign-offs)
- Motion (e.g., unnecessary motion—looking for things, making copies)
- Inventory (e.g., backlog of work—in your inbox, in piles on the floor)

Lack of flow contributes to the creation of many of these wastes, in ways that we discuss in this chapter.

The tool of 5S, which we covered in Chapter 2, makes problems and abnormalities in your work visible and enables you to focus on the value that you're creating for customers. Improving the flow of work enables you to deliver higher-quality work more frequently. When you're focused on creating flow for your work, there is a greater likelihood that you'll finish the day having created value for your customer, instead of thinking, "Where the #*@%^! did my day go?"

There is another advantage to creating flow in your work: a profound psychological benefit. Serendipitously (and conveniently) for us, the Polish psychologist Mihaly Csikszentmihalyi has coined the term *flow* to describe the mental state of a person who is fully immersed in what he or she is doing. Flow is characterized by a feeling of energized focus and full involvement in the activity, whether it's a sport, a conversation, a hobby, or work. It's the feeling of being "in the zone," of being so involved in the task at hand that you lose track of time. Classic batch-and-queue work conditions, with all their rework and interruptions to deal with other tasks, are not at all conducive to psychological flow. They pull us out of the activity at hand and prevent us from "disappearing" into it. By contrast, when value is made to flow continuously in your job, it creates the conditions necessary for psychological flow.

At the risk of sounding as though I'm peddling some sort of 19th-century elixir that will cure all your ailments ("Dr. Markovitz's Magical Flow Potion"), flow will make for both better-quality work and better-quality mental health. But how do you increase flow of your own work, when it's not a simple, repetitive process?

The key is to reduce the variability and complexity of your job by improving the following types of tasks: (1) daily work processes; (2) routine, repetitive work; (3) creative work that can be transformed into routine work.

Daily Work Processes

Processing Your Work: The 4Ds

In a manufacturing setting, the flow of work is both visible and tangible; workers can see the work-in-process inventory building up behind them, and they can see their colleagues farther down the line standing idle. Production line workers don't have the option of leaving tasks undone. They must handle the work as it comes to them, or the line stops. (Or, it requires significant effort in the management system to keep the line moving, but the point is the same.)

But, you don't have that visual cue, and that makes receiving, processing, storing, distributing, and tracking the intangible information and tasks that comprise your work a formidable job. That information comes in the form of e-mails, voice mail, paper memos, or brief conversations in the hallway ("Hey, Bob, can you update the costing for our new Kevlar-reinforced escargot forks?"), and it can be overwhelming. Without a standard process for handling these tasks in an efficient and timely fashion, they pile up until the total quantity of tasks is overwhelming—which usually leads to more procrastination in dealing with them. As a result, project deadlines slip, coworkers wait idly for information, and business processes grind to a halt. Waste—called *muda* in Japanese—floods the system.

In contrast to the products moving down an assembly line, when your work stops flowing, you can't see it—and you won't know about it until your boss or your customer asks you for the second (or third or fourth) time for the report. So, how can you ensure that you're on top of all that work? How can you keep value flowing to the customer?

Applying the "4 Ds" to your work is one part of the answer. (Visual management is another, and is addressed in the next chapter.) When you dive into your paper or electronic inbox, you have to apply one of these 4Ds to each item (eliminating procrastination as a legitimate course of action, of course):

- **Do** it: If it can be completed in less than two minutes, do it right then and there.
- **Delegate** it: If there's someone better suited to handle it, because they have more knowledge or time, delegate it.
- **Designate** it: If it's a more complicated and time-consuming issue, schedule time for it in your calendar or task list at a later date.
- **Discard** it: If it's irrelevant or insignificant, discard it.

When you apply the 4Ds to your incoming work, nothing returns to the inbox. And, even though the value you create still remains intangible and often invisible (in contrast to the value moving down an assembly line), the discipline of the 4Ds ensures that value always moves forward toward your customer. Figure 3.1 will give you a good idea of what this process looks like.

The following are a few examples of how you would actually practice the 4Ds:

- You get an e-mail from your assistant asking for permission to take a day off next week. Because you can make a decision on this in less than two minutes, you **do** it now. Look at your calendar, check to see if there are any conflicts, and reply.
- You find the latest weekly industry newsletter in your mailbox, but your work schedule over the next four days prohibits you from reading it. **Discard** (or **dump**) it in the garbage. Now.
- Your boss sends you an e-mail asking you to determine the effect on the length of patient stay by playing *You Are My Sunshine* on the public address system every morning at 8 a.m. You **delegate** this to someone on your

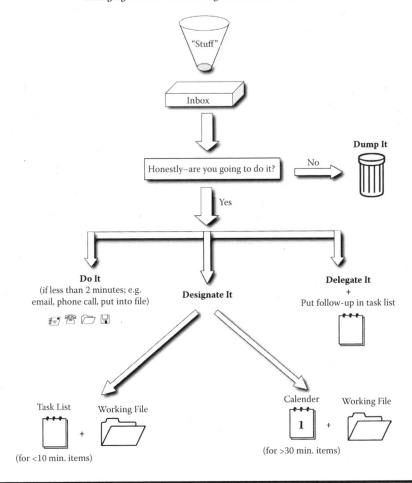

Managing Workflow: Processing Information with the 4Ds

Figure 3.1   4Ds workflow.

team who is better at this kind of research and ask this person to have the information for you by Wednesday. You also move the original e-mail from your boss to a task list with a start date next Wednesday (or flag it for follow-up on Wednesday)—this will remind you to follow up on the date it's due.

■ The travel department at the company is helping you arrange flights for a business trip next month. They're supposed to have an itinerary for you to review next Monday. You **designate** time for a phone call in your task list next Monday to ensure that they're still on top of it.

■ A colleague has asked you to review a manuscript. It's going to take 45 minutes to read and make comments, but you won't have the time for it this week. You **designate** time for it in your calendar (next Thursday, from 3 to 4 p.m.) and put the manuscript into the appropriate working file. (In other words, you get it off your desk and put it someplace where you can find it when you need it. Refer to Chapter 2 on 5S for how to set up working files.)

You may remember that in the section on electronic organization in Chapter 2, I talked about moving all the e-mail you don't need to do anything with into a processed mail folder. I also suggested that you leave all the e-mail that did require follow-up in your inbox. Here—the designate step of the 4Ds—is where you deal with it. Microsoft Outlook, Lotus Notes, and Gmail/Google Calendar all provide easy ways to move messages from your inbox into the calendar or task pad, effectively designating a date and time to work on each task. I won't go into the specific keystrokes for moving mail out of the inbox, but there are many Web sites that demonstrate the various techniques. There are also add-on programs like Add To Calendar[3] that create this functionality for the BlackBerry®.

Remember, you're working in a value *stream*, not a value *lake*. The product or service that the customer (internal or external) needs must flow forward. You can't let it back up in your inbox, in a pile of papers on the floor, or some vaguely remembered promise that you made to your colleague while passing in the hallway. Anything you do that doesn't move the work forward is, by definition, waste. Rigorous application of the 4Ds ensures that the value flows forward instead of getting stuck at your literal or metaphorical workstation.

The $327 Million E-mail

Although the practice of the 4Ds seems simple enough to do, it's worth thinking about how easy it is to violate it. For example, do you ever read and reread e-mails without acting on them? (That includes reading them and marking them as unread so that you don't forget to, um, read them again.) Each time you read something without moving the task forward—without adding value—you've created waste, even in a process that has been *kaizened* to death by an army of Six Sigma galactic master black belts.

And this waste can be large—really large. Huge, in fact. To wit: In 1999, the NASA Mars Climate Orbiter burned up as it began orbital insertion around Mars. The propulsion system overheated because the spacecraft dipped too deeply into the atmosphere of the planet. The story that made the headlines was that the error was due to a mismatch between Imperial units and metric units: The Lockheed Martin engineering team used Imperial units, NASA used metric, and someone failed to make the (very simple) conversion. Oops.

After a full investigation, Carolyn Griner, retired deputy director of NASA Marshall Space Flight Center, said that a simple, *unanswered* e-mail about the correct measurement units with no follow-up resulted in the missed orbit.[4]

Now, it's true there were errors all along the chain that resulted in this failure. But imagine if the person receiving the e-mail about the measurement units had made a habit of the 4Ds when handling this e-mail: The person would have **designated** a specific time in his or her calendar to address the problem before he or she began the tricky process of orbital insertion (most likely in a meeting of the key engineers). Unfortunately, in the absence of this process for dealing with incoming information, the person probably looked at it and decided to get back to it later. Or perhaps the person didn't even read it—maybe the overwhelming volume of daily mail caused the person to miss it entirely (as any of you with several hundred unread messages in your inbox understand). In any event, the critical e-mail disappeared into the vast forest of unanswered messages littering this inbox, and the mission ended in failure.

Oh, yes, regarding the huge waste, the cost of the spacecraft was $125 million. The total cost of the project was $327 million. (And that was in 1999 when $327 million still meant something.)

When you have a multitude of tasks you could be doing at any one time—and you do when you're supporting multiple value streams—there's a real danger that you'll lose sight of key deliverables and won't appropriately prioritize value-creating activities. Making a habit of the 4Ds improves the flow of your work and ensures that you're working on the right thing at the right time. It enables you to act methodically and quickly on your incoming work, rather than jumping aimlessly from one item to the next. In conjunction with using the calendar or a kanban as a signal for your work, it also dampens the reflexive urge to firefight, and keeps you focused on the work that creates the most value.

Worst First

All work is not created equal—and that's not just because some of it is value added and some is non-value added. There is a significant psychological component as well: Some of it you like, and some of it you loathe. And that's important because it's harder to do the work you hate.

If you're a parent, you know to make your kids eat their brussels sprouts first, before you allow them to even sniff the brownie for dessert. You know that if they eat the brownie first, it will take them forever to eat their sprouts: They'll push them around the plate, or they'll "accidentally" drop them on the floor until you finally throw them (the kids, not the sprouts) out of the kitchen. Even if they do finally choke down the sprouts, there's a kind of "time dilation"—it will have taken them much, much longer to eat them, and thus the entire meal, than it otherwise would have.

However, when you put the sprouts first and the brownie second, the brownie is no longer just dessert. It's also the reward for eating the sprouts.

Unfortunately, we are like our own children.

Left to our own devices, we'll also eat our brownies first, and we'll not get to the sprouts. Which is to say that we do the stuff that's easy (e-mail, for example) or the stuff that we like, and we avoid the hard or unpleasant jobs completely—or at least until we have to, when the deadline looms over us like a malevolent cloud. And, like children pushing around their vegetables, when we finally start doing the unpleasant job, it takes us longer than it otherwise might because we interrupt ourselves with e-mail, phone calls, coffee breaks, or anything that is better than what we do not want to do.

Knowledge workers have flexibility in choosing when to do a particular task. It's this flexibility that permits us to pro-crastinate, leads to the waste of waiting, and causes the value stream to stop flowing.

From a Lean perspective, procrastination is unacceptable. The customer doesn't want to wait for your product or service for any reason—even one that is so fundamentally human. You can be sure that your customer—whether that's your boss, the Securities Exchange Commission, or a frustrated patient—is not interested in paying you to push your veggies around your plate.

So, to improve flow, do the worst thing first. When you arrive at the office, before you check e-mail, before you look at the Oscar fashions—before you take care of whatever you find easy or fun—commit to spending a certain amount of time working on the really difficult or unpleasant stuff that's hanging over your head. Hold the easy, more enjoyable stuff until later. As with the brownies, use the promise of the work that's more fun as a reward for dealing with the hard stuff first. Whether you spend 15 minutes or 2 hours doing the worst thing is relatively unimportant. By dealing with it first, you'll minimize the overall time required to dispose of the task.

Now, your work is highly variable; the type, volume, and speed of the tasks and projects that get unceremoniously dumped on your plate change constantly. It's not always easy to identify the "worst" thing, and even if it were, it's not always a simple matter to carve out time first thing in the morning to deal with it.

Yet there is a real benefit to incorporating this kind of work process into your schedule. Predictability helps improve flow, whether it's for production in a factory or the back office. "Worst first" helps to increase the predictability of your work sequencing, and in so doing reduces the potential for non-value-added procrastination. You'll also feel better, and that shouldn't be ignored.

My Story: No Flow = No Business

I break my work down into three major areas: consulting, marketing, and selling.

I love consulting: Working with clients and helping them improve is one of the great joys of my life.

I enjoy marketing. Promoting myself by writing articles for magazines and blogs comes to me pretty easily because I was an English major in college and spent many years learning to write.

However, I don't like selling. I'm not a natural at it, and it's still a blow to my self-esteem when a prospect says "no" to hiring me.

When I first started my company, I would have a list of sales calls that I had to make each day. I dreaded making those calls. So, invariably, the first thing I would do on arriving at the office was check e-mail. That time suck usually cost me about an hour or 90 minutes. Then, continuing to procrastinate on those sales calls, I would read the various magazines, blogs, and articles that I had put aside over the previous few days. I would check e-mail again. Then, some writing—anything to avoid those calls. By then it was time for lunch, and why bother calling at lunchtime?

After lunch, I'd have to check e-mail again and do some more reading. And take care of some office administrative scut work. And check e-mail again. Finally, I would be ready to make those calls … except that it was now 4:30 p.m. Prospects on the East Coast were already out of their offices, and prospects on the West Coast were hoping to go home soon and didn't want to talk to me. So, I would put the sales calls on hold until the next day and the next. Each day, and each hour, I'd find something else, *anything* else, to do instead of making those calls, and I would always find something else to do. Whether it was important or not is another issue. (Needless to say, this is a very bad way to run a business but a very good way to run a business into the ground.)

The problem for me was the flexibility I had in my schedule. I procrastinated on these tasks because I *could*. Worst first mandated making my sales calls first thing in the morning and removed that flexibility. Without the opportunity to vary my work, I handled the unpleasant task first and handled it quickly. Even more important, with the sales calls out of the way, I found that I accomplished all those other tasks more quickly because I was avoiding the subtle time dilation that procrastination creates.

One Thing at a Time—Please

It seems axiomatic that concentrated, focused, uninterrupted work is the best way to do a task well. In that sense, you could consider it essential to flow.

Yet, it's remarkable how many people insist on trying to manage their work by trying to multitask. (For that matter, it is remarkable just how many job postings specifically state that the "ability to multitask is a must.") Current neuroscience uniformly and convincingly proves that multitasking is a myth, and a dangerous one at that. Short of doing the simplest physical activities concurrently—walking and chewing gum comes to mind—humans aren't built to do two things at once. Anything that places a greater cognitive demand on the brain than, well, chewing gum, requires dedicated focus and attention to do it well.

(A quick point here: The multitasking I'm referring to is the attempt to do two things simultaneously, like talking on the phone while reading an e-mail. I am not referring to doing one activity while waiting for another process to finish—for example, cooking dinner while the laundry is running or preparing a budget while waiting for your boss to review a space-planning proposal.)

David Meyer, a cognitive scientist and director of the Brain, Cognition, and Action Laboratory at the University of Michigan, says, "Multitasking is going to slow you down, increasing the chances of mistakes. Disruptions and interruptions are a bad deal from the standpoint of our ability to process information." René Marois, a neuroscientist and director of the Human Information Processing Laboratory at Vanderbilt University, commenting on the results of a study he published in the journal *Neuron*, said that "a core limitation [of the human brain] is an inability to concentrate on two things at once."[5]

In fact, the brain doesn't actually do two things at once; rather, it rapidly (or actually, not that rapidly) switches between two activities. The result of this attempted multitasking, as numerous studies showed, is poor performance due to "dual-task interference." The interference can be significant: Participants in a University of Michigan study who were asked to write a report and check e-mail at the same time took one and a half times longer to finish than individuals who did the same two tasks sequentially.[6]

Walter Kirn described the effects this way:

> Multitasking messes with the brain in several ways. At the most basic level, the mental balancing acts that it requires—the constant switching and pivoting—energize regions of the brain that specialize in visual processing and physical coordination

and simultaneously appear to shortchange some of
the higher areas related to memory and learning.
We concentrate on the act of concentration at the
expense of whatever it is that we're supposed to be
concentrating on. ... In reality, multitasking slows our
thinking. It forces us to chop competing tasks into
pieces, set them in different piles, then hunt for the
pile we're interested in, pick up its pieces, review the
rules for putting the pieces back together, and then
attempt to do so, often quite awkwardly.[7]

It's no surprise that our ability to focus on a single task
without interruption is waning. To some extent, an increase in
interruptions is an inevitable result of the larger, more complex organizations of today. Managing sprawling enterprises
requires more team and individual interactions, and dotted-
line relationships in matrix structures abound. Cubicles have
replaced private offices. Moreover, the pervasiveness, ease,
and zero cost of e-mail, instant messaging (IM), and SMS
(short message service) have exacerbated the situation by
encouraging communication, even when it's not valuable.

What is a surprise, however, is the extent to which interruptions define our workdays. Gloria Mark, a researcher at
the University of California at Irvine, studied workers at two
West Coast technology firms. She found that employees spent
only 11 minutes on any given project before being interrupted.
Even worse, each 11-minute project was itself broken into
even shorter 3-minute tasks, like answering e-mail messages
or working on a spreadsheet.[8]

More important, interruptions keep us from completing
the task at hand effectively. Mary Czerwinski, a scientist at
Microsoft Research Labs, found that 40% of the time, workers
wander off in a new direction when an interruption ends, distracted by the technological equivalent of shiny objects. As the
New York Times put it, "The central danger of interruptions,

Czerwinski realized, is not really the interruption at all. It is the havoc they wreak with our short-term memory: 'What the heck was I just doing?'"⁹

Looking at psychological flow from a Lean perspective, it's obvious that distractions and multitasking have to go. Not only are they stressful, but also they ruin the flow of the value stream and lead to all manner of Ohno's seven wastes—perhaps most significantly, errors (defects). At Kaiser South San Francisco Medical Center, for example, nurses were able to reduce medication administration errors by 47% simply by educating staff about the dangers of distraction and providing nurses who were passing medications a bright orange vest that communicated clearly that the nurse should not be disturbed.¹⁰

Serial Tasking

"Serial tasking" is the solution to this problem. It is a way to bring your work process under control, reduce waste, improve flow, and allow you to continually improve performance. Here are some ideas on how to move toward serial tasking:

■ Group similar tasks into blocks of activities to reduce the time lost to switchover. Do your budgets, your drawings, your contract reviews, your e-mails, and so on at one time rather than switching between them.
■ Establish meeting "corridors" for all people in the company—essentially office hours when you and others are available to meet with colleagues. Obviously, during emergencies people will disturb you, but this will reduce the nonurgent interruptions. Even better, set up standard check-in periods during the day for the people with whom you interact the most: When they know they'll get to see you for 10 minutes each morning and afternoon, they'll be more willing to wait. If the nature of your job necessitates nearly constant collaboration and

communication, then reverse this idea: Set aside one or two hours per day for completely uninterrupted work.

■ A company I know has a totally open floor plan. It doesn't have any offices, and the cube walls are low—about chest height—so there is no privacy. They've found a simple solution: Each person has made two paper signs. A green sign says "open," which means they are available to talk. A red sign has a time written on it—in other words, "Do not disturb until___o'clock." (Interestingly, no one ever interrupts an assembly-line worker at Toyota. In fact, it's precisely the opposite: They have resource buffers [team leads and group leads] who respond to problems that a worker has in order to insulate downstream workers from interruption. The entire system is set up to prevent workers from being interrupted.)

■ Turn off e-mail alerts to reduce distractions. Even if you don't respond to an e-mail immediately, the very act of reading (or hearing) the alert fractures your concentration. Learn to deal with e-mail in blocks—twice a day, four times a day, once an hour—whatever is the appropriate interval for you and your company.

■ Reduce self-inflicted interruptions by keeping a notebook or pad of scratch paper next to your computer. When you suddenly remember an e-mail you have to send or a phone call you have to make, don't do it. Instead, quickly write it down on the paper and go back to what you were doing. This may sound trivial, but it's not. The problem isn't the one e-mail that you plan to send—it's the 14 new, unread messages that are sitting in your inbox that you won't be able to resist. You'll end up reading them, answering them, and losing yet another 45 minutes to e-mail instead of keeping the flow of your work moving.

■ Set "service-level agreements" that support your work. With e-mail in particular, there's an assumption that because a message can be sent immediately, it must be answered immediately. And in fact, we've trained people to expect instantaneous response. But more often than not, people don't really need an immediate answer; they need a predictable response—say, within a few hours or within the day. To address emergencies effectively, set up a "white list" for certain people and an e-mail rule that notifies you when those people send you a message. Better yet, have people use the phone for urgent issues. After all, if the issue is that critical and time sensitive, asynchronous communication tools like e-mail probably aren't the best option anyway.

Let legendary management philosopher Peter Drucker have the final word on this subject:

> To be effective, every knowledge worker, and especially every executive, needs to be able to dispose of time in fairly large chunks. To have dribs and drabs of time at his disposal will not be sufficient even if the total is an impressive number of hours.[11]

Lowering the Water Level

Toyota uses a powerful metaphor in its approach to process improvement; the company talks about "lowering the water level" in the production process to expose the rocks hidden below the surface of the water. Reducing the resources (time, money, inventory) in the process—lowering the water level—exposes the "rocks" that represent all of the hidden costs and waste in production. Only by revealing those rocks can you improve the process and reduce the waste.

In your case, the key resource is time. Having too much time to do your work hides the waste and inefficiencies in your own process.

Now, most people would deny they have too much time to do their work. Not too many people are taking three-martini lunches anymore or leaving the office right at 5:00 p.m. On average, Americans only take about 79% of their vacation time, and 24% of people check work e-mail and voice mail while on vacation.[12] And with cell-phone- and Crackberry-addled days, nights, and weekends, it seems as though there is an infinite torrent of work.

But, here's the thing: Your cell phone, smartphone, and general willingness to work late and on weekends are part of the problem, not the solution—counterintuitive, but true.

Yeah, yeah, I can hear you now: "If I didn't have my smart-phone, if I didn't put in a few hours on the weekend, I'd never get on top of everything I need to do. I'd be buried. I'd probably get fired."

The fact is, if you had less time for your work, you'd get it done more quickly. You'd be *forced* to get it done faster. Parkinson's law—work expands to fill the time available for its completion—recognizes this unfortunate reality of human nature. And, if you don't believe it applies to you, think about what I call the vacation paradox: Even though you never seem to be able to get all your work done on a regular day, on the days right before you go on vacation, you somehow manage to crank through all your daily work plus a good chunk of the backlog of stuff that has been moldering on your desk for the past month.

What's going on? It's no secret: When you're short on time, you hunker down and work more efficiently. You reduce the waste in your work process so that you can get stuff done. There's no choice because you're on the plane to Aspen or Amsterdam tomorrow.

But, to go back to the Toyota analogy, when the water level—your time—is high, there's no need to reduce ineffi-ciency. Why bother removing the waste in your work habits when you can just stay at the office an hour later or get it done over the weekend? That's the nefarious aspect of living on your smartphone 24/7, your willingness to work on weekends and give up your holidays: You effectively raise the water level by increasing the amount of time you have to accomplish your work.

When a factory doesn't have inventory (of parts) to mask production problems, workers are forced to solve the problems in the production process. If you cut your inventory (of time), you'll be forced to address the root causes of inefficiency in your own production process.

To go one step further, the need to stay late or work on weekends should actually trigger an analysis of what's gone wrong with your production process. If you've been successfully managing your work in 45-hour weeks and it suddenly spikes to 55 hours, you shouldn't just passively accept that "things got busy." Rather, you should analyze the causes of the increase. There might be things that you're doing differently that led to the increase. Or, there might be a change elsewhere in the company that slowed the process (in which case, you'll want to find a countermeasure for that change).

Of course, there's no "right" number of hours you should be working. But in the spirit of continuous improvement, you should always be striving to reduce the resources (i.e., time) that you need to produce your work. Restricting the inputs will force you to find creative ways of reducing your work effort. As Yoshihito Wakamatsu explained in his book *The Toyota Mindset: The Ten Commandments of Taiichi Ohno,*

> Instead of saying "Purchasing more machines will fix the problem," say "How can we fix the problem with the same number of machines?" Instead of saying "If I had a bigger budget we could grow at x%," say "With the same amount of budget, how can we grow at x%?"[13]

As part of your work process improvements, try to reduce the amount of time you spend on certain activities. Can you shorten weekly staff meetings from 60 minutes to 45 minutes? Can you leave the office 30 minutes earlier one day per week? Can you spend 15 fewer minutes per day processing e-mail? Can you reduce the number of reports you have to generate or reports you have to read?

Like so much of Lean thinking, the concept of lowering the water level exposes problems and forces you to confront them immediately. With less time to spend on these activities (or just less time in the office), you'll have to find and eliminate the waste in the way you operate—and free up more time for the value-added work your customer demands.

The First Step, but Not the Last

This list of improvements to your daily work processes is nothing more than a beginning. Your work environment is unique, and the way you work is by definition idiosyncratic. You'll almost certainly need to modify—and add—to this list as your job changes, as the technology you use changes, and as *you* change. In keeping with Lean thinking, there's never one, best, final solution. Your job is to continually examine the way you work to see if there's a better way—if there's a way to reduce the inefficiencies and waste in your work habits and to continue improving.

Routine Work: Your Job Requires More than Just Creative Genius (Unfortunately)

No matter what kind of work you do, it comprises both creative, unpredictable elements, and mundanely repetitive tasks. While it may be hard (or impossible) to bring flow to the creative areas of your job, it's certainly possible to bring flow to the more repetitive areas. After all, managers have to do performance reviews. Doctors have to dictate cases. Medical technicians need to do preventive maintenance on hospital equipment. Artists have to inventory and buy paints (and pay the rent on time). Actors have to go to the gym and get regular Botox treatments. This work isn't particularly exciting, but it's eminently predictable, and it needs to get done.

What's surprising, though, is how often these tasks are left to languish. Rather than being processed systematically so that they can be taken care of in the normal course of business, this transactional work lies about people's offices like a beached whale, consuming mental space and stinking up the joint. This work isn't sexy, generally not much fun, and not urgent (until, of course, it is). But when transactional work finally comes due, *everything* stops—colleagues, customers, patients, and family all take a back seat to the completion of these relatively unimportant tasks.

For example, I once worked with Keiko, the chief financial officer of a large law firm in San Francisco. She knew that every month she had to present key financials to the executive committee. In fact, she knew the exact date of every monthly meeting for the whole year. Yet, somehow, preparations for the meeting always fell to the last minute and ended up consuming a full day and a half right before the deadline. This procrastination frustrated her boss, who wanted the opportunity to review the presentation a few days before the meeting— and it frustrated Keiko's direct reports, who couldn't get any help from her for a day and a half each month.

This situation is the antithesis of flow. It is the worst kind of batch-and-queue process, and it needlessly creates waste and stress. With better flow, Keiko would be able to delegate some of the work to her staff, deliver the report to her boss on time, and increase her accessibility to customers within the firm.

Joe's Story: A Kitchen Timer Yields Perfect Results

About three years ago, the president of Joe's small company asked him to manage the approval of all of the nonpayroll checks each week. These were usually a stack of 80 to 120 invoices each week for everything from raw materials to office supplies, utility payments to food for meetings, and even major consulting agreements.

The approval policy for these expenditures at the company required higher levels of approvals for larger expenditures. Joe's job was to make sure those approvals were all done correctly—his review was the final one before checks were cut. But with the high volume and variability of these checks (a $30 office supply check could be right next to a $30,000 legal bill), Joe needed a system to ensure that he would not miss something.

He realized early on that boredom, familiarity, and loss of focus was a real issue. How could he fight that tendency and maintain attention? And, how could he provide feedback to the company president about expenditures?

He developed a simple system. (All the best systems are simple.)

He asked the clerk who prepared the invoices each week to run off a simple list of all the transactions, with just the payee and the amount to be paid. He also asked the clerk to format the list by segmenting each group of 10 invoices with a simple blank line.

Joe determined that by working within the policy constraints of the company, it would take him about seven minutes to review 10 invoices. Some invoices were handled quicker than others, of course; the water bill never varied much. Other invoices required scrutiny to see if the sign-off was correct and if the purchase order for an oddball piece of equipment in the lab really matched the invoice. But, overall, seven minutes per 10 invoices was about average.

He set a kitchen timer when he started to process the invoices. At the first break of 10 invoices, he wrote the actual time on the list. If it took him less than seven minutes, he put a plus sign next to it. If it took him longer, he wrote a minus sign and determined why it took longer. It was okay if he had a genuine question on one of the invoices. If he was simply daydreaming (which, he admitted, happened), he gave himself a metaphorical slap in the face and started on the next 10.

Joe did the same thing at the next 10 and for each subsequent group of 10.

How did this help flow?

For one thing, it kept him on pace for standard work. When he got a stack of invoices, a quick scan of the list told him how many groups of 10 he had and therefore how much time he needed to allocate to the job. It also alleviated boredom because he knew that if he gave the invoices the right level of scrutiny, seven minutes was about right. Finally, it provided immediate feedback, just like any takt[14] time measurement does—on a stack of 90 invoices, Joe had nine distinct pieces of feedback.

Find the Predictability

If you look closely at your own work, you'll undoubtedly spot areas of predictability amidst the variability of your own job. These areas hold the potential for improved flow. In Joe's case, for example, he knew that each week he had to block out one hour to approve the nonpayroll checks. Putting that in his calendar as a standing appointment ensured (or at least made it more likely) that he would complete the course with a minimum of disruption. Keiko could improve the flow of her monthly presentation by carving out small blocks of time to prepare the report. In fact, breaking the work into smaller pieces with a regular cycle might even enable her to delegate pieces of the job to her staff. Becoming aware of these opportunities and taking advantage of them will result in a greater ability to deploy your skills and creativity in solving unforeseen problems.

Excessive Choices = Paralysis

As a knowledge worker, you have a nearly infinite amount of work—and an infinite amount of flexibility in what you can work on at any given moment. Although this flexibility is rewarding and stimulating, it has a significant downside: It can lead to decision-making paralysis about *what* to do during each day. That paralysis impedes flow and wastes a significant amount of time.

Sheena Iyengar, a professor at Columbia Business School, conducted a famous experiment in which she showed the effects of having too many choices.[15] She put jars of jam on tables in a supermarket—different flavors in groups of 6 and 24—and offered samples to shoppers. She discovered that the table with 24 attracted more visitors, but the table with 6 jams prompted a greater proportion of people to buy (30% of those who stopped at the 6-flavor table bought a jar, while only 3% at the 24-flavor table made a purchase)—a 10-fold difference in action.

The problem, as Iyengar pointed out, is that when confronted with too many choices (she believed that the optimal number is about seven), people shut down and default to the easiest, most familiar, course of action—which is often doing nothing. If you have ever been faced by a wall of toothpaste (Fluoride? Tartar control? Sensitive tooth? Whitening?) and struggled to make a decision, you know the feeling. Or think about the time you had to make your 401(k) investment allocations or choose among cell phone plans; the number of options and variables are so numerous they make decision making difficult.

Now, consider the daily plight of a knowledge worker. With dozens of projects and tasks in process, it's difficult to choose which to work on. You arrive at the office, stare at a to-do list as long as your arm, and then, overwhelmed by choice, default to the easiest option: checking e-mail, or getting a cup of coffee, or just doing the simplest, easiest, fastest (but not necessarily most important) task. Your ability to act intelligently is compromised by the sheer number of choices you have before you (Figure 3.2) This is one reason that a to-do list doesn't work.

The solution to this problem is to engage in what Columbia University social theorist John Elster called "self-binding." Like

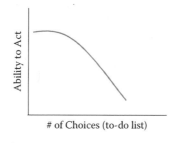

Figure 3.2 Options and the decision-making process.

Ulysses lashing himself to the mast of his ship to prevent himself from succumbing to the Sirens' song, people can make the choice to limit their choices. By restricting your choices through planning and "predeciding" your activities and putting them in your calendar, you can limit both the time and effort it takes to get your work done.

Transforming the Creative into the Transactional

A final way to improve flow is to transform complex, creative work into simple, "transactional" tasks that can be done easily. Checklists are a perfect example of this concept. They ensure that individual steps within a complicated process are both remembered completely and done correctly.

NASA astronauts and ground operations use checklists for all space missions. Since the crash in 1935 of a prototype B-17 bomber, pilots use checklists when taking off and landing planes—the process is just too complicated, and the downside risk is too great, to rely on mere memory. Checklists are increasingly finding their way into medicine as well, dramatically reducing infection and mortality rates where they're being used. Dr. Peter Pronovost has been leading the way in this area, as Atul Gawande reported in *The New Yorker*:

The checklists provided two main benefits, Pronovost observed. First, they helped with memory recall, especially with mundane matters that are easily overlooked in patients undergoing more drastic events. (When you're worrying about what treatment to give a woman who won't stop seizing, it's hard to remember to make sure that the head of her bed is in the right position.) A second effect was to make explicit the minimum, expected steps in complex processes.[16]

Your work may have less riding on it than the lives of patients or passengers, but there's no doubt that there is complexity in your work that, if eliminated, would improve flow and reduce waste. Chip and Dan Heath wrote about the benefits of checklists in business:

> Even when there's no ironclad right way, checklists can help people avoid blind spots in complex environments. Has your business ever made a big mistake because it failed to consider all the right information? Cisco Systems, renowned for its savvy in buying and absorbing complementary companies, uses a checklist to analyze potential acquisitions. Will the company's key engineers be willing to relocate? Will it be able to sell additional services to its customer base? What's the plan for migrating customer support? As a smart business-development person, you'd probably remember to investigate 80% of these critical issues. But it would be inadvisable to remember the other 20% *after* the close of a $100 million acquisition. (Whoops, the hotshot engineers won't leave the snow in Boulder.) Checklists are insurance against overconfidence.[17]

Checklists reduce ambiguity and uncertainty, thereby allowing faster action with less deliberation. They provide the same benefit that habits do in setting free, as William James put it, the "higher powers of mind" for creative thought.

Checklists improve flow in one other significant way: They dampen the tendency to multitask in favor of serial tasking. In a rapidly changing, always-connected work environment, serial tasking may sound heretical. At the very least, it probably sounds slow and inefficient. And yet, serial tasking leads to a smoother flow of work (and value). What we often forget is that the most complex activities are composed of individual actions—done one at a time. A good analogy might be the performance of an elegant prima ballerina in *Swan Lake*: Her dance is composed of a series of individual movements—turns, steps, and jumps—done in sequence, one at a time. But when they're linked together, they create a seamless, flowing whole. The same is true for your work. Even if you're not creating an artistic masterpiece, you can nevertheless strive for the same smooth, uninterrupted, flow of work.

Both Transactional and Creative

Checklists don't eliminate the need for creative work, whatever the field. There will always be unpredictable problems and crises that demand quick thinking and improvisation. Indeed, figuring out how to simplify and standardize complicated work so that it can be made transactional is itself part of that creativity. In this regard, it's like Toyota's relentless pursuit of perfection in their processes. Journalist Charles Fishman pointed out how a Toyota factory only *looks* like a car factory: "It's really a big brain—a kind of laboratory focused on a single mission: not how to make cars, but how to make cars better." At Toyota, he explained,

> The work is really threefold: making cars, making cars better, and teaching everyone how to make cars better. At its Olympian best, Toyota adds one more level: It's always looking to improve the process by which it improves all the other processes.[18]

Toyota uses checklists and other tools to standardize the work that can be standardized and uses employee creativity and the higher powers of the mind for continued improvement in their work processes. The same philosophy applies to individual work as well. Transforming creative work into transactional work smoothes the flow of work and enables you to create more value for customers.

Applicable to Almost Any Work

In a previous career, I headed up product marketing for running shoes at a large athletic footwear company. One of my tasks was to review early factory prototypes to ensure that all specs were correct. It's a complicated and important process composed of many steps, and when we missed items in the past, we had to make costly changes after production. We made a checklist (a portion of which is shown in Table 3.1) to reduce the probability of errors—and were pleasantly surprised to find that it actually took us *less* time to complete the prototype review.

Table 3.1   Footwear Prototype Review Sheet

		Comments
Upper		
• Shoelace length	☐	_____
• Number of eyelets	☐	_____
• Tongue length	☐	_____
• Toe reinforcement coverage	☐	_____
• Heel counter height	☐	_____
• Ankle collar height	☐	_____
Midsole		
• Medial density	☐	_____
• Lateral density	☐	_____
• Medial sculpting	☐	_____
• Forefoot undercut	☐	_____
• Heel bevel	☐	_____
Outsole		
• Flex grooves	☐	_____
• First metatarsal head coverage	☐	_____
• Lateral heel design	☐	_____
• Trusstic density	☐	_____

Next Steps

You can improve the flow of your work by reducing its variability and complexity. Even though there will always be a large element of unpredictability, that's okay; what we're trying to do is address the controllable factors that create waste and inefficiency.

To a certain extent, 5S and techniques to improve flow are concepts both to make the value in your job more readily apparent and to reduce the waste that occurs in the course of doing your work. The ideas in the next chapter will help you stay focused on your value-creating activities, ensuring that you do the right thing at the right time.

- Apply 4Ds to all paper in your inbox.
- Apply 4Ds to all e-mail messages in your inbox.
- Make a recurring calendar appointment for 9 a.m. (or whenever you come to work): "Worst First."
- Turn off e-mail alerts.[19]
- Make a sign for your door (if you work in an office): "Do Not Disturb Until ___ O'Clock
- While you are doing other work, keep a notepad next to your computer to record phone calls you want to make or e-mails you want to send.
- Schedule specific times for processing e-mail.
- Create a checklist for one of your repetitive processes.

Notes

1. Multitasking is actually a bit of a misnomer. A better word for the activity might be what productivity coach Dave Crenshaw called "switch-tasking" because we don't really do two things at once. Like a computer, we actually serial task, switching rapidly between the things that demand our attention. It's in this switch from one activity to another that we lose time and increase the likelihood of errors. The full effects were well detailed in studies by David Meyer at the University of Michigan, Rene Marois at Vanderbilt University, and Clifford Nass at Stanford University.
2. *Lean Thinking*, James Womack and Dan Jones, Free Press, New York, 15.

3. "Add To Calendar 1.0.8: Free Download." http://handheld.soft-pedia.com/progDownload/Add-To-Calendar-Download-46921.html.

4. From a speech delivered at the American Institute of Aeronautics and Astronautics, St. Louis Section, March 2001 dinner meeting.

5. "Slow Down, Brave Multitasker, and Don't Read This in Traffic," Steve Lohr, *New York Times*, March 25, 2007.

6. "The Limits of Multitasking," Klaus Manhart, *Scientific American Mind,* December 2004, 62–67.

7. "The Autumn of the Multitaskers," *Atlantic Monthly*, November 2007.

8. "Multitasking Drives Workers to Distraction," *ABC News*, January 27, 2005.

9. "Meet the Lifehackers," by Clive Thompson, *New York Times*, October 16, 2005.

10. "Decreasing Disruptions Reduces Medication Errors," Debra Wood, NurseZone.com, http://www.nursezone.com/Nursing-News-Events/more-news.aspx?ID=18693.

11. *The Effective Executive*, Peter Drucker, HarperCollins, New York, 29.

12. "2009 International Vacation Deprivation™ Survey Results," Expedia.com, http://tinyurl.com/yzfzlqp.

13. *The Toyota Mindset: The Ten Commandments of Taiichi Ohno*, Yoshihito Wakamatsu, Enna, Bellingham, WA, 2009, 52.

14. No, that's not a typo. Takt time is derived from the German word *taktzeit,* which refers to the pace of production needed to meet customer demand. In automobile manufacturing, for example, cars are assembled on a line and are moved to the next station after a certain time—the takt time. Takt Time = (Net Available Production Time/Required Output Rate).

15. "When Choice Is Demotivating: Can One Desire Too Much of a Good Thing?" S. S. Iyengar and M. Lepper, *Journal of Personality and Social Psychology,* 79, 995–1006, 2000.

16. "The Checklist," Atul Gawande, *The New Yorker*, December 10, 2007.

17. "Heroic Checklist," Dan and Chip Heath, *Fast Company*, February 14, 2008.

18. "No Satisfaction at Toyota," Charles Fishman, *Fast Company*, December 19, 2007.

19. Here are directions for three of the most common e-mail programs. For Outlook: Tools > Options > Preferences tab > Email Options > Advanced Email Options > clear all checkboxes in the "When new items arrive in my inbox" section. For Lotus Notes: File > User Preferences > Mail > clear the "Show a pop-up" checkbox in the "When new mail arrives" section. For Apple Mail: Mail > Preferences > General > select "None" for the "New Messages Sound."

Chapter 4

Visual Management

Introduction

We've already established what 5S can do for you. By cleaning out the physical, digital, and mental junk that accumulates in your office and in your mind, you're better able to see the value and the waste in your work and spot any abnormalities or errors. This is important stuff. Unfortunately, it's not enough to help you manage the torrent of intangible work that is coming at you from all directions.

We've also seen how improving the flow in your work processes can help you reduce waste. Having a process for dealing with your work, cutting down on interruptions, grouping similar tasks, using checklists—all these techniques enable you to work more efficiently.

However, neither of these tools is particularly good at bringing clarity to the murky mess of ongoing tasks and project work. When you have multiple demands for your time and attention at any given moment, how do you choose what to do next? You require another tool that enables you to diagnose current conditions quickly and easily, maintain a smooth flow of effort, and keep value flowing to your customer.

You need visual management.

What Is Visual Management?

"Visual management," or "visual controls," is an important component of Lean thinking. Visual management systems are designed to provide instruction; convey information; give immediate feedback; expose abnormalities in a process or work area quickly; and demonstrate progress toward a goal. In other words, visual management makes readily apparent that which is normally invisible, tacit, or assumed.

A shadow board for tools is an excellent (and simple) example of this function. If you've ever hunted for tools in a toolbox, you'll immediately understand the appeal of the shadow board. In one brief glance, you can tell where to place and find items.

A shadow board also helps to identify a missing tool immediately (Figure 4.1). That may not seem terribly important at work when all you're dealing with is the Kessler vacation file, and an extra two minutes doesn't really matter. However, it is extremely valuable if you're working in, say, a prison. The shadow board in Figure 4.2 was used in the kitchen at Alcatraz to help officers keep track of large knives and cleavers that otherwise might have, um, gone missing.

With some creativity, you can create visual controls for information as well. The tape on these binders in a hospital office (Figure 4.3), for example, provides immediate feedback regarding whether all the files are present and in the right spot.

These three examples demonstrated how visual controls help manage static, physical things. But they are also used to track processes, such as the status of a production line. Many factories have whiteboards displayed near an

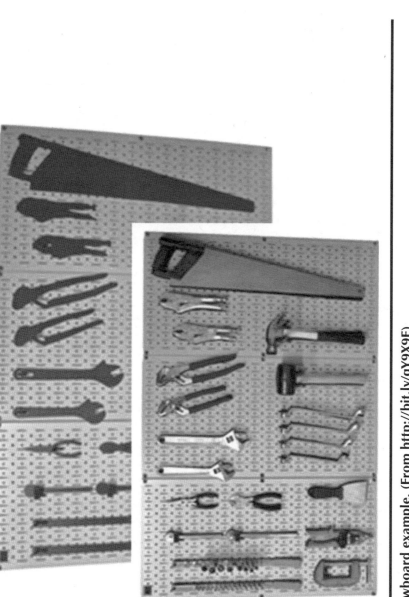

Figure 4.1 Shadowboard example. (From http://bit.ly/qY9X9E)

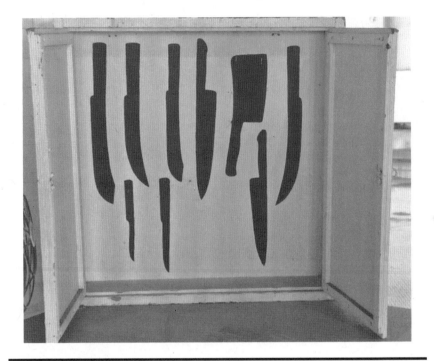

Figure 4.2   Shadow board used in kitchen at Alcatraz. (From http://1. USA.gov/PULQpd)

Figure 4.3   A hospital laboratory's three-ring binders. (From *Lean Hospitals*: *Improving Quality, Patient Safety, and Employee Engagement*, **Second Edition, Mark Graban, 2012, p. 86.)**

assembly line listing hourly production targets, actual results, and reasons for any discrepancies.

But use of visual management systems is not limited to physical production lines. They have a nearly infinite number of uses in any kind of environment. Figure 4.4 is a visual management board that tracks a software development project—a "knowledge production line."

Figure 4.5 shows a board that tracks the progress of small-scale purchases in a large company. The board in Figure 4.6 is used by someone at home to assign household chores to the family children.

Each of these visual management examples is quite different, but all are effective in reducing what Gwendolyn Galsworth called the "information deficits" in the workplace that lead people to ask the same questions repeatedly, miss deadlines, and make all manner of mistakes (particularly the household chores board).

The Irony of "Out of Sight, Out of Mind"

The value of visual controls goes beyond the communication of information among people and departments. These controls are also a powerful method of managing your *own* work, which is essential because you can have information deficits even with yourself. In other words, you often lose sight of the important things you have to do, and the deadlines for those things, even if you have a really good memory—after all, if you can't see the work, you can't be sure that it hasn't been lost.

Some people respond to this challenge by piling the physical elements of their work up on the desk, the floor, the credenza, the file cabinet—pretty much any horizontal surface that's not a pizza. They carefully and laboriously write and rewrite lengthy to-do lists (or several), stick a flock of Post-it

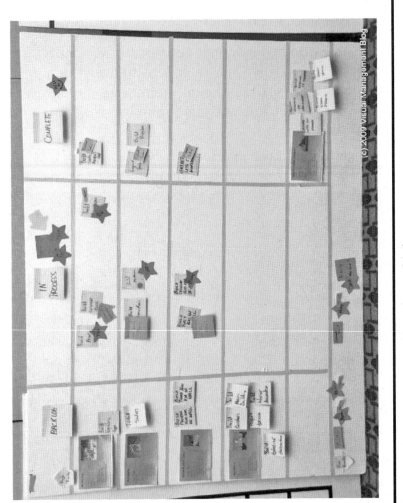

Figure 4.4 Software production kanban. (From http://bit.ly/pqv9VV)

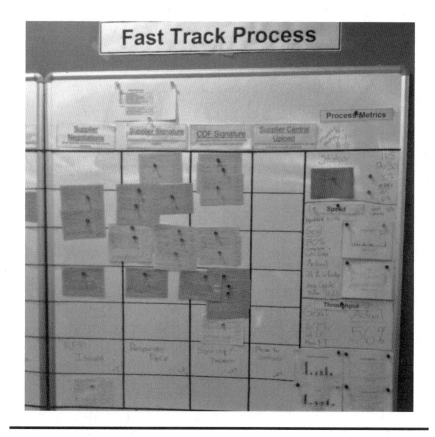

Figure 4.5   Purchasing group kanban.

notes to the desk and computer, and install the latest whiz-bang iPhone productivity applications. Intuitively, they realize that they need some visual cues to help them manage their work. They resist putting anything away because "if it's out of sight, it's out of mind." But with visual cues scattered everywhere, it's impossible to stay on top of all the information flows and spot any problems. Where do you look for what you need? Ironically, by keeping everything in sight, it all eventually becomes invisible.

The key to effective visual controls is to create a system that makes your work—your projects, your ongoing commitments, and your responsibilities—easily visible so that you

Figure 4.6   Family kanban. (From http://bit.ly/ruSJP6)

can, at a glance, know what's supposed to be done. Visual management for the knowledge worker is no different (conceptually) from visual management for a factory worker: You should be able to see your production targets and your actual production results.

Why All Those To-Do Lists Don't Work

Fact: The amount of work you have to do is infinite. Even if you were physically able to work 24 hours a day, every day, you'd never get to the bottom of your to-do list (or your e-mail inbox). There will always be one more meeting to attend, one more problem to solve, or one more e-mail to write. Not to put too negative a spin on the situation, but clearing that list is truly a Sisyphean chore.

Fact: The time you have to do this infinite amount of work is quite clearly finite. Whether you work 40, 50, or 110 hours per week, there is a limit to how much you can accomplish each week. Just as there's a physical limit to the throughput on a manufacturing line and a limit to how many jets can take off from LaGuardia airport each hour, there's a limit to how much work you can do each week.

Given this reality, you have to treat your time like you treat your money: as a limited resource that must be budgeted. And just as you first budget money for the essential things in life—food, shelter, peanut M&Ms—you've got to budget time for your most important work.

The thing is, you can't properly allocate time to your really important stuff if you only log your work in a to-do list or a pile of Post-it notes. Neither of them captures or displays the vital bits of information you need: When is each task due? How long will it take? And the corollary: how much time do you have available? If you can't answer these questions, you can't intelligently decide whether you can afford to spend time filling out employee reviews, revamping the nurse staffing schedule, or doing trust falls and ropes courses at the executive team-building retreat. Until you can see the time required to do X, you can't assess the opportunity cost of doing it. Because when you're doing X, you're quite clearly not doing Y.

So, what's the answer? How do you make your work visible so you can ensure that you're getting the right stuff done?

Living in the Calendar

At some point in the past year (and probably even more often than that), you've probably complained that you're always being *reactive* rather than *proactive*. The reason is simple: It's because you constantly "live in your inbox" by keeping it front and center and let the incoming messages drive your work. In doing so, you've essentially ceded control of your daily activities to other people. Other people's issues, questions, and emergencies become paramount.

This is dangerous.

By living in the inbox—by using it to drive your day—you guarantee that your work will become invisible at some point. After all, even if you have a computer screen the size of a Buick, eventually some of your mail will get pushed below the edge of the monitor and disappear from view. Yes, you could of course scroll up and down to spot important messages that have been pushed down, but do you really want to spend even more time in your e-mail inbox, scanning for work that might have slipped through the cracks? That's nothing but waste: waste of overprocessing and waste of motion in Lean terms, not to mention a waste of time, effort, and energy in normal human terms.

It is far better to "live in your calendar" and let your *designated* work drive your actions. (Remember from the chapter on flow that designated work comprises the tasks that you assigned to your calendar or task pad during the 4D processing of your inbox.)

The Calendar as Kanban

Okay, here's another Japanese word for you: *kanban*. Literally, a kanban is a signboard or a billboard. The Lean community uses the term in a broader sense: It's any physical signal that tells an operator when it's time to perform work and produce something. On a production line, a kanban might be a bin holding parts; when it's empty, it's sent back to the previous station to be refilled. In the customer service department of an office, a kanban could be a folder that holds unprocessed orders; when it's empty, it gets sent back to the preceding step to be refilled. In a hospital pathology lab, it could be a special tray that holds frozen sections waiting to be read.

A kanban is useful for changing the flow of work and information from a "push" system to a "pull" system. A push system is one in which the upstream process sends materials to the downstream process whether or not the downstream process needs it. A pull system is one in which the downstream process requests materials when it's ready, and that request is a trigger for the upstream process to begin work. Push systems create all manner of waste. Pull systems reduce it. Pull systems help create flow.

An example of a push system in a factory is when the guys making bumpers crank out hundreds of units even though the guys installing the bumpers farther down the line only need two bumpers at a time. In a bank loan-processing department, a push system occurs when the people doing the initial credit check work out of sync with the team doing phase two of the analysis, creating a large pile of work waiting to be processed.

In the office world, where electronic information is the coin of the realm, push systems are often harder to see. Regularly scheduled status report meetings are classic examples of information push: People have to prepare information that often isn't needed at that moment by most of the members of the team. That's pure waste—waste of time, waste of processing, and waste of motion.

Now, imagine that instead of these meetings, which so often drag on for hours, the team used a centrally located status board to indicate what each person is doing that day or week. Team members update the board daily, and the manager (or anyone else) can check the board on a regular schedule. Instead of trapping workers in a conference room for two hours with stultifying PowerPoint presentations, people get the information that they need, when they need it.

By scheduling your own work in your calendar—and not just all the meetings that you have to attend—you've essentially turned it into a kind of kanban that signals when it's time to pull work out of your buffer inventory (your working files, which we discussed in the chapter on information 5S). When you use the calendar in this way, it triggers your work. It's a signal that ensures you begin working on it at the right time—not too early, when you have other commitments due, and not too late, after the deadline has passed.

There are two major benefits of a kanban that make it worth adopting. First, it enables you to match your production capacity to your customers' demand. There's no point in promising to finish the pharmacy reorganization by Tuesday if you are completely walloped with revising the budget this week. Second, it enables you to pull work forward at the right time. Rather than relying on your (leaky) memory to address a problem, the kanban brings that job to the fore when you need it.

Of course, with the overwhelming flood of commitments, requirements, and meetings, it probably doesn't feel as though you have the ability to pull anything; you're just struggling to keep your head above water and get the barest minimum done. But the truth is that whether you schedule your work or not, you're already choosing (consciously or unconsciously) to act on certain things today and postpone other things until later. However, it's far better to make this process conscious and transparent so that you know what work needs to be done at any given time—and what work doesn't need to be done.

The Calendar and the Task Pad

A calendar is well designed for large chunks of work that consume an hour or more. It's not so good, however, at handling short tasks of 10 minutes or less. If you were to put all your follow-up e-mails and phone calls in your calendar, you'd rapidly run out of space for the bigger projects you're working on. And, electronic calendars in particular are not particularly well suited to creating a five-minute appointment. So, how do you make those tasks visible, without resorting to a paper to-do list?

Here is where the electronic task pad comes into play: The task pad can hold all short (less than 30-minute) tasks that would overwhelm a calendar, and—more important—it lets you know on which day you are supposed to do those tasks. For example, if you have delegated something to a colleague that is due next Friday, you can put a reminder in the task pad with a *start* date (not a due date) of next Wednesday to check in and see if everything is going smoothly. Now, you've made the work visible: It shows up on the calendar, with all the relevant details, rather than just being a nagging, anxious feeling that you have to do something.

It's worth explaining why you want to set a start date rather than a due date. If you set the start date, the task appears on the day that you are supposed to do the job—not before. If you set the due date, the task appears on your calendar every single day *until* the date the task is due, which means that you have to look at something you're not prepared to tackle for weeks or months—and as I discussed in a previous chapter, that means it will almost certainly become invisible to you. (Or, it will drive you crazy, which isn't much better.)

By using the task pad in this way, you've created pull for your work—because the task pad reminder doesn't show up until next Wednesday, when you're ready to do something about it, you do not have to think about the task until the appropriate date. The work is visible just when you need it to be (Figure 4.7).

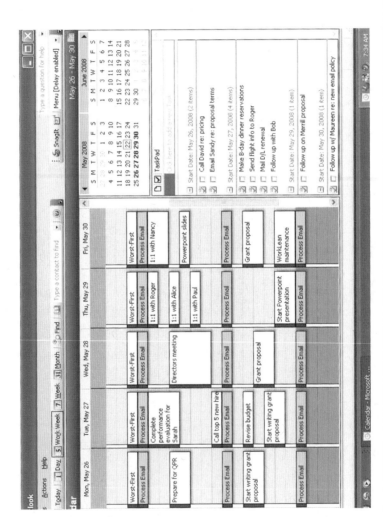

Figure 4.7 Outlook Calendar and TaskPad.

Caution: Don't Treat Your Calendar Like Your Gas Tank

People tend to treat their calendars like an eight-hour version of the gas tanks in their cars—something to be filled completely. If there's five minutes free on the calendar, surely they should schedule something in that slot. After all, they've got a ton of work to do, and they don't want to waste any time.

Here's the problem with that thinking: Without any slack in your schedule, the calendar-as-kanban results in gridlock. Packing your calendar with appointments and work as tightly as cars on a rush-hour freeway means that you can't adapt easily (or at all) to unexpected changes in circumstances. Any slight disturbance in your perfectly arranged calendar causes the whole system to crash. If you've ever sat in a doctor's office for 45 minutes waiting to be seen, you've felt this problem: The doctor's schedule is 100% full, with absolutely no slack. And with no room to move, there's no flexibility. You have got to allow for the inevitable, but unpredictable variability that will enter your day.

The Old Movies Had It Right

Think about a movie with an office scene set in the 1940s, 1950s, or 1960s—or in any event, a movie set in the precomputer era. I often think about the Spencer Tracy/Katherine Hepburn *Desk Set* movie, or perhaps *It's A Wonderful Life*. Now, try to imagine a scene in the executive's office: There's Jimmy Stewart sitting in that tiny chair in front of Mr. Potter's giant black desk, a brass lamp on one side, a phone on the other, and right in the middle of the desk, in front of the chair is ... what? Can you remember? It's a blotter—with a month-at-a-glance calendar on top of it (Figure 4.8).

Figure 4.8 *It's A Wonderful Life.*

The executive, of course, had that calendar front and center because he (and it was always a man) needed to know where he was going and what he needed to do. The telephone—his version of e-mail—was off to the side, ready when he needed it, but not the focus of his work. Big hitters like President Obama have the same setup today (Figure 4.9).

Now, think about your desk. You've got your computer screen front and center—which makes sense, because that's where you do your work—but you probably have your e-mail open and in front of you 80% of your day. That would be as silly as Mr. Potter, or any of those old movie executives, having their phones smack in the middle of their desks. This is what I call living in your inbox.

Remember: E-mail is not really your work (even if it sometimes feels that way). E-mail is simply a communication tool, just like a phone, a telegraph, or a really fancy version of two Dixie cups and a piece of string. If you're a secretary or a

Figure 4.9   President Obama's desk.

receptionist and your job is to answer the phone and respond to e-mail, then fine: Keep e-mail open at all times. But, if your job is a bit broader than that—and if you're reading this book, it probably is—then you should seriously consider keeping your calendar open and in front, instead of your inbox.[1]

Sometimes a Little Inventory Is Okay

The notion of living in your calendar is another aspect of standard work (discussed in the next chapter), and it goes hand in hand with the idea of processing your incoming work with the 4Ds. Once you begin designating dates and times for specific tasks and projects, you've essentially created a production schedule for your work.

I can hear your objection now (at least, if you're a hard-core Lean guy): "A real pull-based system of work would have me responding to the incoming messages as they arrive. Living in the calendar means creating inventory rather than flow."

That's true. This pull system does create inventory. And, if your job entailed working in only one value stream—as it would if you were on an assembly line—then it wouldn't be a good idea.

But, you don't work in just one value stream. As a knowledge worker, you're involved in many value streams at once, with multiple tasks and projects coming at you at the same time, performing very different types of operations (e.g., billing, talking to vendors, preparing budgets, composing ad jingles) for many different customers (your boss, the client, the Food and Drug Administration), often with differing delivery dates. It is an extraordinarily complex environment.

If you were to work on each item as it arrived—just-in-time production, true one-piece flow—you'd inevitably end up creating inventory anyway, and you'd almost certainly miss key delivery dates. Since your incoming work doesn't flow smoothly and predictably, you're guaranteed to have conflicting delivery schedules. So, just as a machine job shop must schedule production based on complexity, delivery date, and duration of production, and just as hospital emergency departments must schedule medical procedures based on severity of injury and treatment duration, you also have to schedule your workflow—and that necessarily means creating work-in-process inventory.

But—and here's the key—you want the calendar to drive the work that you do, not the order in which the job arrives (i.e., the time it arrives in your inbox). The calendar pulls work forward at the right time, allowing you to allocate your resources (time and energy) properly. It enables you to level the load where necessary—for example, shunting aside work when you're in the middle of a crisis with a customer or a product. It allows you to calculate takt time[2] and create fast tracks for predictable and repetitive work, such as dictations or personnel evaluations. It helps you carve out sufficient time for complex, resource-intensive jobs like preparing for a Joint Commission visit or creating a new compensation plan for hourly workers.

You just can't manage your work this way when you live in your inbox.

Lean manufacturers often talk about the "single-minute exchange of dies" (SMED). This refers to the rapid and efficient way of converting a manufacturing process from running the current product to running the next product. The longer the changeover of the tools takes, the more production is lost each day, and the more expensive the overall manufacturing process is.

As we saw in the chapter on flow, your brain is also a machine, and there is a real and significant cost to changing over from one task to another. But, because you're working on many projects at any one time, you'll inevitably have to switch tasks multiple times during each day—and that kind of multitasking seriously degrades efficiency. By using the calendar and task pad to organize and group similar tasks in your schedule, you can reduce the cost of these switches. For example, handling your e-mail in several batches during the day, doing all your writing in chunks, or selecting all the colorways for next season's products at one time helps reduce the cognitive impairment you'll suffer from the switches.

Of Course, Life Never Goes According to Plan

This all sounds good in theory, but of course, life never goes according to plan. You may have designated time Tuesday morning from 9 to 11 a.m. to write a grant proposal, but inevitably, an emergency will erupt and take precedence over the scheduled work. That's okay. In fact, it's precisely *because* something urgent inevitably arises that you need to live in your calendar.

Without a calendar to pull your work at the right time, you run the risk of losing track of that other, less-urgent task. If your product development team has just discovered a major problem with the alignment of two parts on your new product and it takes you seven hours to deal with it, the odds are excellent that you'll forget whatever it is you were supposed to do that day.

The calendar prevents you from forgetting. Simply figure out when you can finish that scheduled task you missed and reschedule it. Acting as a kanban, the calendar will then pull the rescheduled work into the job queue at the (new) right time.

But, what if you can't reschedule it? What if your calendar is so full of work that there's simply no time to take care of it? That situation is often a reality for some people. In that case, the calendar has done you the invaluable service of making that problem visible: You can actually *see* that you don't have the two hours to work on the grant proposal before the submission deadline, rather than being surprised by that realization a few days (or weeks) later. So, you can either delegate responsibility for writing (at least part of it) to someone else, you can choose to create more production capacity for yourself by working on Sunday, or you can determine that it's not that important after all and ignore it.

Regardless of which option you choose, you've at least made the options visible, and the choice conscious, rather than invisible and inadvertent. As I'm fond of saying, if you're going to get run over by a truck, you might as well get the license plate number. The visibility the calendar affords, and your resulting response, helps avoid what George Gonzalez-Rivas and Linus Larsson called the "green-green-red" phenomenon, in which the status of a project is green (everything is on target, no problems) until it suddenly and unexpectedly turns red (it's going to be two months late).[3] And if it's a recurring problem—which you can now see—you have the opportunity to engage in root cause analysis and problem solving so that it doesn't keep happening.

Assessing Personal Production Capacity

When you can see your work on the calendar, you're able to make conscious decisions about what you're going to do and what you don't have time for—being proactive, rather than reactive. You can more appropriately allocate your production capacity to the incoming work that's requested of you so that you ensure faster completion of your tasks.

You're also able to see when you're on task, doing your scheduled work, and when you're off task, tending to emergencies. You can begin to spot trends and ask questions: Are Thursday mornings particularly chaotic? Is the beginning of the month filled with too many meetings? Have you been consistently rescheduling a particular project? Does the handoff to the billing department usually create confusion? You now have the ability to spot problems, find root causes, and create countermeasures.

Living in your calendar doesn't guarantee that you'll be able to do your scheduled work on any given day or week. Life is too chaotic and unpredictable for that. But, it does enable you to discriminate between what you're *actually* doing and what you *should* be doing and, if necessary, implementing countermeasures to help ensure that you keep value flowing as smoothly as possible.

But, What if You're Allergic to Calendars?

Living in the calendar can be tough. Some people are pathologically allergic to that much structure. It feels suffocating and claustrophobic to try to shoehorn all of your work and all of your personal responsibilities into one of those grids. Some people may have jobs that are just too variable and volatile ever to be able to plan what they are going to do at what time. If your job is tech support in your information technology department, you know what I'm talking about: Because you must respond to problems as they come in, you can't structure your day with a calendar. Your schedule is entirely at the mercy of your internal customers.

Okay.

Forget about using the calendar as a kanban. Instead, make your own "personal" kanban to manage your work. Jim Benson, chief executive officer of Modus Cooperandi and leader of the "personal kanban" movement,[4] has written about how a personal kanban improves your ability to manage multiple projects and infinite task lists by preventing you from becoming overcommitted and causing the system to grind to a halt.

As Jim explained it eloquently:

> All too often, we equate "free time" with "capacity" and assume we have the ability to fit in more work. In this case, we are not unlike a freeway.
>
> A freeway can support from 0–100 percent capacity. But when its [load] extends beyond 65%, it begins to slow down. When it reaches 100% [load], it stops.
>
> Capacity is a horrible measure of throughput. … If your brain is a highway and you are filling yourself with work, after a while you start to slow down. Your mental rush hour gets longer and longer. You find yourself struggling to accomplish even the simplest tasks.
>
> Simply because you think you can handle more work-in-progress does not make it so.[5]

The Simpler Method: The Personal Kanban

A personal kanban allows you both to visualize the amount of work you have and to limit the amount of work in progress. In this respect, it functions just like the calendar. However, because work is not tied to a specific time or date, the personal kanban is much more flexible than a calendar. Moreover, the kanban easily allows you to see all your work at one time, in one place.

Consider the task board in Figure 4.10. You've probably seen something similar before. The owner of this task board abandoned it for three reasons. First, it didn't identify the discrete, interim steps of each project, so it effectively masked the work he had to do. Second, it didn't tell him what he was working on (or what he was supposed to work on) at any given time: Work was "on target," but that didn't tell him whether he was waiting for something or had to do something to keep it moving forward. Finally, the information was redundant with the project files kept on the shared drive.

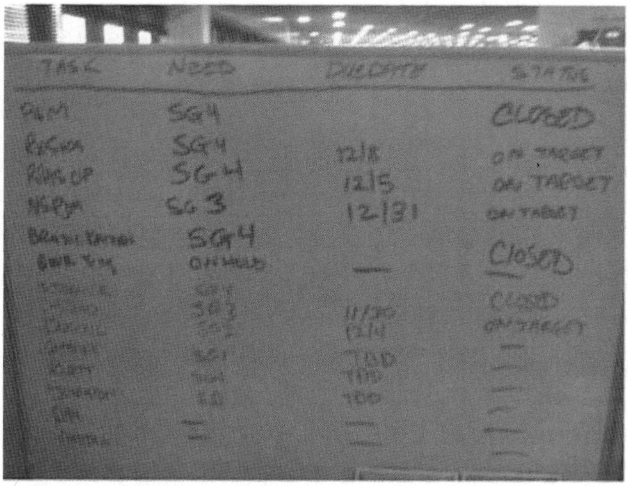

Figure 4.10　Typical task board.

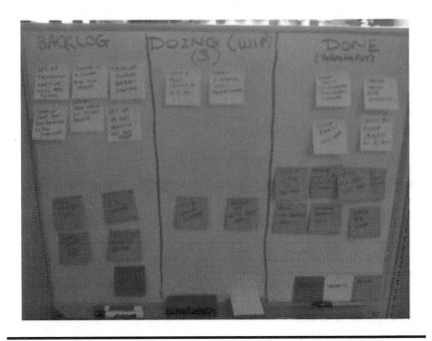

Figure 4.11   Personal kanban.

He eventually moved to the kanban in Figure 4.11. This kanban was superior to the task board in several ways. It helped him establish a backlog of individual tasks. Limiting his work in progress to three or four items at a time improved his level of focus on tasks associated with projects. The kanban improved his ability to prioritize his work. The different color Post-it notes enabled him to easily categorize his work as project related, administrative, or personal. Finally, the kanban reduced interruptions by providing the necessary information to his supervisor and peers about what he was working on.

Four Easy Steps

Jim Benson explained that there are four steps to creating a kanban for your own work:

First, establish your value stream—the flow of work from the moment you start to when it is finished. The simplest value stream possible is backlog (work waiting to be done), doing (work being done), and done.

Second, establish your backlog. All the work you need to do that you've not done—that's your backlog. Put all your tasks on Post-it notes. Jim warned against sweeping things under the rug: "Don't lie to yourself. Your first backlog-fest should be a painful experience. You should, at some point say, 'God, there's way too much of this.'"

Third, establish your work in process (WIP) limit. The WIP limit is the amount of work you can handle at one time—per day or per week. The goal is to prevent you from leaving work half-done because of overcommitment to projects. It also ensures that, in Jim's words, the "highway of your brain" does not exceed 65% capacity and start to slow down.

Fourth, begin working and pull work from left to right on the kanban, from one stage of the value stream to the next. The key point, of course, is that you can't move an item from the Backlog into the Doing column until you move an item from the Doing column to Done (Figure 4.12).

The Incredibly Flexible Kanban

Versatility is one of the strengths of the kanban. Tasks can be sorted by size or by category just by changing the color or size of the Post-it note. The kanban can include repetitive tasks as well—for example, making phone calls to clients, or updating the results of a long computer run. For people who are addicted to e-mail, limiting the number of Post-its for e-mail—say, a total of three—provides a visual cue that you're only allowed to check e-mail three times per day.

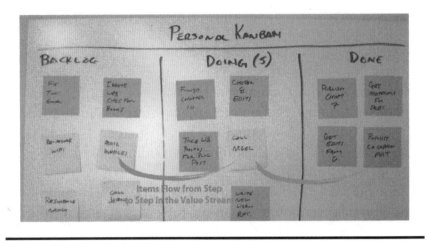

Figure 4.12   Kanban flow from personal kanban. (From http://www. personalkanban.com/pk/wp-content/uploads/2009/08/JimBenson_02-Aug.-23-18.17.gif.)

Even the backlog doing done categories can be changed to suit your environment. For example, a small-business owner managing several product development projects set up his kanban to fit the "plan-do-check-act" paradigm that Lean thinkers use for all their work (Figure 4.13).

Other Types of Visual Management

Visual management tools are a wonderful way of delegating work and managing projects as well. Most people have seen a Gantt chart or a Microsoft Project report that shows a series of dependent and independent tasks, all flowing toward the on-time completion of a goal.[6] Gantt charts do have their uses, of course, but most of the time they're just overkill. Most organizations I've visited spend more time updating the information in the Gantt chart than actually doing the work. In addition, they're so elaborate that, to paraphrase Winston Churchill, "Those charts, by their very length, defend

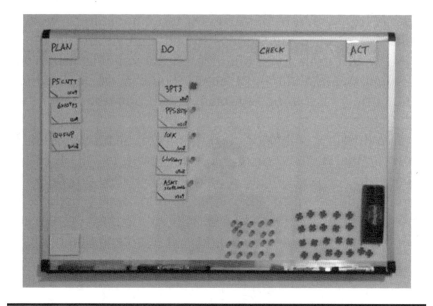

Figure 4.13   Jon Miller kanban. (From http://bit.ly/r7U603)

themselves against the possibility of ever being used." If you're building a nuclear submarine and need to coordinate the installation of the plutonium reactor core and the surrounding lead shielding, by all means use a Gantt chart. But if your projects are somewhat simpler, maybe you could get by with something less fancy.

What you need is a system that makes the work each person is doing visible while indicating whether their task is on target. A simple kanban that lists all staff and their tasks within the workflow eliminates the need for lengthy status updates and reduces repeated questioning about the status of the work. Want to know where people stand? Go to the board and look for yourself. Need to know whether someone is in trouble? Use green and red pins or flags to indicate whether the process is on time or falling behind.

Reflexive versus Cognitive Systems

Perhaps the greatest benefit of visual controls is the conversion of a "cognitive system" into a "reflexive system" for triggering work. That's a lot of heavy jargon, so let me explain.

A cognitive system is one that requires a person to make a mindful, conscious decision about when and how to act in a given situation. A doctor who has to remember to check on a patient's lab results is an example of a cognitive system: The doctor has to rely on personal judgment to guess when the results will be ready to read. The doctor might guess wrong, of course, which leads to all kinds of waste—if the doctor is too early, multiple checks will be needed, and if the doctor is too late, the patient and other medical staff are forced to wait. The system relies on human discretion and memory to keep everything moving.

By contrast, a reflexive system is based on rules and doesn't require human judgment to keep work moving according to plan. It either uses flags or "trip wires" to move work forward automatically or relies on a preset time or routine that causes a person to look for the flag. A simple example is a reorder card for office supplies. In a closet with boxes of printer ink cartridges, place a card on top of the last box with the reorder quantity; when the card is visible because all the other cartridges have been used, it signals to everyone that it is time to place an order for more ink. There's no need for anyone to think about when or how many boxes to order.

The hospital lab cognitive system discussed could be converted into a reflexive system by using a kanban; for example, when technicians complete lab results, they could signal with a rack of green cards that results are in, and an assistant rounding on a 30-minute schedule could pick up the results and deliver them to the doctor.

Now, think about your average day: You're getting scores of e-mails, receiving a pile of action items at meetings, and you're delegating work. By definition, not all of this work can be done at once; most items have different deadlines and milestones, and they generally require follow-up at different times.

Before you read this book, you probably put all those items in a to-do list, or (in the case of e-mail) you left them in your inbox so you could follow up with them later. Of course, as I described, neither of these approaches helps you figure out when to do each of these tasks, and as a result, you have to scroll up and down the list continually to decide which to do now. This is cognitive system hell.

By using the calendar as a kanban or by building a personal kanban, you're creating a reflexive system that allows work to flow smoothly forward without requiring you to make decisions all the time about what to do next. The calendar or the personal kanban is the trip wire that indicates which work needs to be done next Tuesday morning and reminds you to follow up with your subordinate on Friday; you don't have to remember it. The advantage to this type of reflexive system, of course, is that you don't have to think quite so much. This is reflexive system paradise.[7]

Reducing Ambiguity

In the end, visual management systems—whether you use your calendar or some sort of kanban—reduce the ambiguity you face as a knowledge worker. Instead of dealing with an amorphous blob of stuff to do, you have diamond-hard clarity about the specific tasks that need to be done and when they need to be completed. You reduce the waste caused by continual assessment and reassessment of your infinite task list and replace it with focused, value-creating activity. Visual management allows you to use time—the one truly nonreplenishable resource—as efficiently and wisely as possible.

Next Steps

- Move all of your tasks, projects, and ongoing commitments into your electronic calendar and task pad.
  - Tasks that will take less than 30 minutes go into the task pad or to-do list. Remember to assign a start date to these items.
  - Tasks that will consume an hour or more go into the calendar.
- Experiment with a simple personal kanban. (You don't need to buy a whiteboard; you can simply tape a few pieces of paper together and pin it to the wall.)
  - Make three columns: Backlog, Doing, and Done.
  - List all your projects—not individual tasks—on separate Post-it notes. Put them all in the Backlog column.
  - Move three projects into the Doing column. This represents the work you are handling now. The tasks that you put into your calendar and task pad should match up with the projects in the Doing column. If they don't, rearrange one or the other to eliminate the conflict.
- When you finish a project, move it to the right into the Done column.

Notes

1. An excellent way to do this is to start your day by looking at your calendar—not your e-mail. In fact, one of the most nefarious aspects of Microsoft Outlook is the way it defaults to

starting up in your inbox. You can change this default setting by following these steps: Click on Tools > Options > Other > Advanced Options > Browse > Calendar.

2. See the explanation of takt time in the chapter on flow.

3. *Far from the Factory,* George Gonzalez-Rivas and Linus Larsson, Productivity Press, New York, 2011, 83

4. Information about personal kanbans is at their Web site: http://www.personalkanban.com/pk/.

5. Taken from Modus Cooperandi InfoPak 2 slideshow at http://www.personalkanban.com/pk/personal-kanban-101/ (accessed February 6, 2011).

6. A Gantt chart is a horizontal bar chart that shows the tasks of a project, when each task is supposed to take place, and how long each will take. The Gantt chart also shows which tasks are independent and which tasks are dependent on prior steps.

7. More accurately, this is really a semireflexive system. When your boss drops a superurgent, number one, top-priority project on your desk, you'll have to decide whether that really supersedes the superurgent, number one, top-priority item that he dropped on your desk *yesterday*. There's no algorithm that can make that decision for you. You'll always be making those types of decisions and trade-offs. Moreover, the system still requires you to decide up front when you're going to do something—there's no blanket rule that can automatically assign a time or date to handle an issue. Nevertheless, a kanban is effective in converting at least some of your work into a reflexive system.

Chapter 5

From Bad to Good, and From Good to Great

It is not the strongest of the species that survives, nor the most intelligent, but the one most responsive to change.

—Charles Darwin

Like an Air Traffic Controller

Think about the way you started your morning today. If you're like most people, the first thing you probably did was check e-mail. And if you are like most people, what started out as a well-intentioned—and brief—triage of your mail turned into a giant time suck in which 90 minutes disappeared with your head up your, um ... , inbox before you realized it.

Or perhaps you came to work and hammered through the budget revisions the chief financial officer (CFO) had requested. You were on a tight deadline, and you knew you didn't have time to waste.

Or maybe you had an early meeting with a colleague who was having difficulties with a project that you're leading.

Or maybe you returned a call from the nurse supervisor who needed information about a new procedure you are doing in the hospital.

Or … , well, the list of things that demand your attention is pretty much infinite. When you walk into your office, you're like an air traffic controller, with multiple demands on your attention at any given moment. That means that there are many different ways you can structure your daily work; what, when, and how you work can—and usually will—vary from day to day.

But why is there so much variability in how you start your day? For that matter, why is there so much variability in how you manage the whole of your day? Is that the best way to work? When you arrive at your desk in the morning, or when you return to it after a meeting, you have a load of new information that you have to receive, store, process, and distribute—but do you have a well-defined method? Or do you just hack away at it, reading a few e-mails, checking a couple of voice mails, and thumbing through some of the papers littering your desk until your next meeting? Do you have a standard way of dealing with incoming work and customer requests? Or do you just take care of your boss first or the person who is screaming the loudest? Is this haphazard way of processing information and work the best way to handle your job?

Is it possible that there's a right way—or at least a better way—to do *your* job? Yes, yes, I know: Because you're a software engineer, a surgeon, or the executive director of a nonprofit, your job is inherently more variable than that of someone doing the same repetitive task every day, like the guy who receives parts at the loading dock of a factory. And it's true: Your work is more unpredictable and the types of "goods" that arrive in your inbox or are dropped on your desk are more heterogeneous than those that the loading dock guy deals with.

But you know how on some days you get a bunch of important work done, while on others, despite working your tail off, you feel as though you've accomplished nothing? What if that feeling isn't just due to external circumstances? What if the way you work, and how you structure your day, is partly responsible for how efficient you are?

Here's a concrete example: The pathologists at a large cancer center I've worked with sit in their offices, analyze cases (slides of tissue samples), and then report to the surgeon and oncologist what they've found. Reading slides is labor intensive and requires focus. Unfortunately for the pathologists, they seldom get to focus; when technologists have a new batch of slides to be read, they walk into a pathologist's office, say hello, and drop the slides on the doctor's desk. That interruption breaks the pathologist's focus and usually forces him or her to start reading the slide from the start—after all, the pathologist wants to be sure to do a thorough job. That means it takes significantly longer to get through the pile of work than it should.

But why do the technologists have to interrupt the pathologists? The slides don't have to be analyzed at that moment. It's only because—and this sounds silly—there's no other place to put the slides. The solution was absurdly simple: We placed cardboard boxes outside the pathologists' office doors so that slides could be left there and retrieved later. This simple change helped them read more cases each day and reduced the likelihood of errors.

The Twin Pillars of *Kaizen*

Kaizen is the Japanese word for "continuous improvement." It's a pretty widely used bit of business jargon these days—after all, no organization wants to be known for standing still. Organizations usually focus on the "improvement" element of kaizen, but the real secret is the "continuous" piece of kaizen. Anyone can make a one-time improvement in a process. What separates the Lean approach to work is the notion that improvement is part of daily work, not merely something to be done when you have an obvious problem or when you have a little free time.

Now that you've identified the value you create; eliminated the obstacles to creating value through 5S; improved the flow of your work to produce value more efficiently; and created visible management tools to help you focus on the value-adding activities—how do you keep from backsliding to the old ways of working? What kind of system cues you when you're not working Lean and, in fact, prompts you to improve?

This kind of system rests on two pillars: PDCA (plan-do-check-act) and standard work. The abbreviation PDCA essentially means "the scientific method." It's shorthand for the process of observing and measuring a situation, formulating a hypothesis, testing the hypothesis against reality, and adjusting as necessary. PDCA is controlled experimentation (Figure 5.1).

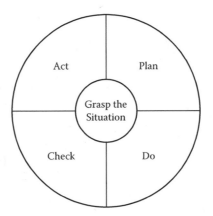

Figure 5.1   The PDCA wheel.

As a simple example, a hospital might hypothesize that having doctors remove their neckties will reduce infections in a hospital (unlike doctors' hands, neckties don't get washed or sterilized, so they are a virtual petri dish of bacteria):

Plan:	From April 1 to 30, doctors will not wear ties at work.
Do:	Doctors come to work without ties from April 1 to 30.
Check:	Compare hospital infection rate during this period with the previous months and check for improvement.
Act:	If infection rates drop, then continue the policy; if they stay the same, reject or modify the hypothesis and formulate another one (e.g., lab coat sleeves may be a bigger contributor to infections).

In this example, the value of PDCA is obvious. In business practice, however, most companies spin in a pointless plan-do-plan-do-plan-do cycle (or even worse, a do-do-do-do cycle), like autumn leaves in a river eddy; they never stop to check and act, with the result that they have no idea whether their actions were effective.

Think about the last time your company did a reorganization to improve communication and colloboration between departments: Did it work? How do you know? Do you have any measurements (quantitative or qualitative) to indicate whether the reorganization was successful? If you're an entrepreneur, think about your decision to start blogging: Has it helped customers find you? Do you have more business? How do you know if you should keep blogging or try a different approach to marketing communications? If you're a salesperson and you've tried a new sales technique, how do you know if it helped you close more deals? Only PDCA can tell you.

It is the tool by which real improvement is made because it removes the "gut feel" from the evaluation and replaces it with a controlled experiment and facts.

Bob Emiliani, a professor at Central Connecticut State University, has used PDCA over the past 13 years to improve the design and delivery of his classes. Bob hypothesized that one of the drivers for the high "defect" rates (i.e., bad grades) was the standard practice in college of giving students only two exams during the semester—midterms and finals. He thought that by giving the students smaller batches of information and testing them on it more frequently (plan), he could improve their mastery of the material. He tried that during one semester (do); compared the grades to previous years and surveyed the students (check); and then modified the assignments and lectures appropriately (act/adjust). Students had a better grasp of the material and their grades were higher. There was no ambiguity here: Bob ran a controlled experiment, learned what worked, and made changes that directly resulted in improvement—better student grades.

However, while PDCA is necessary for sustained improvement, it's not sufficient. Gains in performance, quality, and profitability inevitably erode over time as internal and external conditions change. To sustain improvement, you need standardized work.

Standardized Work

Standardized (or standard) work is an organization's definition of the best way to do a certain task. In a manufacturing job, for example, standard work will tell people where to stand, how to grasp a part, which screw to tighten first, and which gloves to wear. In a hospital, standard work will tell pathologists how to slice and stain a biopsy sample. In a law firm, standard work will guide attorneys in how to draft a contract or how to make a closing argument. Standardized work does not—cannot—cover all contingencies during the course of a workday. But it does address the repeatable, predictable tasks and processes in which workers engage.

The goal of standardized work is not to dehumanize employees or to make them replaceable by low-cost temporary staff in Mumbai. (In fact, managers and the people doing the actual work develop the standards in concert. This cooperation avoids the ludicrous rules and policies that management often foists on employees and that inevitably leads to workarounds to accommodate better ways of working.) The goal of standard work is simple: to reduce variability in production and eliminate defects.

Standard work is not static. It changes over time because it's a codification of the best way to do a job—but only at a given moment. Employees continually experiment to find better ways to work based on changes in tools, in materials, in technology, and so on. If a new process works better, then it's adopted as the new standard—until a worker finds a better, safer, faster way to perform the operation. Leeches and bloodletting used to be the medical standard for curing sickness; now, antibiotics are the standard. Coronary bypass surgery—an open-chest procedure—once was the standard for curing clogged arteries. Now, the procedure is done in a minimally invasive manner with a stent.

Standard work is the foundation for truly sustainable improvement because it allows you to isolate and control the variables that you are going to tweak to improve. After all, how can you tell you've improved, and how can you tell what change made a difference, if you don't have standard work? In fact, it's not going too far to say that without standardized work, there can be no real kaizen.

The classic drawing in Figure 5.2 shows how standard work and the scientific method (PDCA) work together to enable true, sustainable, kaizen. This approach is an entirely different

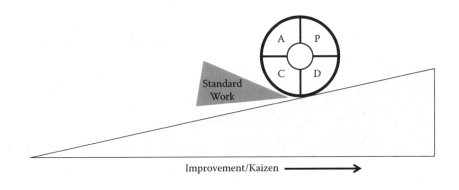

Figure 5.2   Standardized work and kaizen.

paradigm from the typical improvement model, in which you learn new programs or enroll in classes. In this approach, standard work acts as the "wedge" that keeps the PDCA wheel from rolling back down the slope of improvement. Think back to the checklists I talked about in the chapter on flow; they're really nothing more than a specific kind of standardized work. And once the new, better processes have been adopted and institutionalized, a new round of PDCA and improvement can begin.

To put it more concisely, you discover and codify the best way of doing a task. You make this best approach your daily way of work. Then, the fun starts—you get to improve this process. You now have a foundation for sustainable excellence.

Creative Types Need Standard Work, Too

At this point, you might be thinking that the creative nature of your job, and the variability within it, means that you cannot standardize anything—au contraire. Think, for example, of an artist—the epitome of creativity, right down to the beret perched jauntily on his head. But, if you look closely at his paint palette, you will notice something interesting: The colors are not randomly placed. In fact, they're *always* in the same place to make it easier and faster to find the right color when it's needed. In other words, part of an artist's standard work is mixing the colors in the right spot on the palette. This standardization is important because if you're lying on your back painting the ceiling of the Sistine Chapel, the last thing you want is to have to hunt continually for the yellow.

Think of the way a doctor gives a standard physical exam: The doctor checks your ears, eyes, and nose in the same sequence every time; has a predefined sequence when listening to your lungs with a stethoscope; and even asks the same health history questions in the same order every time. That's standard work, and it ensures that the doctor doesn't miss any important clues to your health.

My wife, an interventional radiologist, recalls learning to evaluate every chest X-ray in the same order: first bones, then heart, and finally lungs—every X-ray, every time. This habit minimized the possibility that a finding in one area could distract her and cause her to overlook others. The sequence for any of these tasks is in and of itself irrelevant. The important point is simply to have a system so that the actions and processes are done the same way every time.

When I worked as a middle-school English teacher, I had standard work for the way I taught grammatical constructions: I would introduce the rules the same way and have the students practice them the same way every time. Although that may sound like drudgery (and I suppose for some of the kids, it was), it enabled me to teach the concepts faster, to reduce the variability in how they were learning, to keep the quality of the teaching constant, and gave me more time to add creativity and fun to other aspects of teaching. It was a standardized system for transferring knowledge from me to them.

Irrespective of whether you are doing an assembly job in a factory or writing an advertising jingle, there are elements of your work that can also be standardized. PDCA and standardized work, writ large, are essential tools for improving processes in an organization. Writ small, they are essential tools for helping you to improve your own personal work, regardless of what is happening in the organization around you. Taken together, they enable you to improve the way you currently do your job by changing the fundamental content of the work.

These two pillars of kaizen are nothing less than a foolproof mechanism for improvement: define standard work, analyze and eliminate the gap between the current state of affairs and the desired state of affairs with PDCA, make new standard work, and then begin the cycle again—lather, rinse, and repeat.

Creating Mental Capacity for Improvement

There is another huge benefit to standard work—a psychological one.

The American psychologist, William James, believed that the creation of habits was essential to productivity and efficiency. Habits are, in a sense, nothing more than standard work that has become automatic and reflexive. If you'll bear with me (and his turgid, 19th-century prose) for just a bit, you'll see he was actually quite eloquent on the subject:

> Habit is the flywheel of society, its most precious conserving agent. The great thing, then, is to make our nervous system our ally instead of our enemy. We must make automatic and habitual, as early as possible, as many useful actions as we can, and guard against growing into ways that are disadvantageous as we guard against the plague. The more of the details of our daily life we can hand over to the effortless custody of automation, the more our higher powers of mind will be set free for their proper

work. There is no more miserable person than one in whom nothing is habitual but indecision, and for whom the lighting of every cigar, the drinking of every cup, the time of rising and going to bed every day, and the beginning of every bit of work, are subjects of deliberation. Half the time of such a man goes to deciding or regretting matters which ought to be so ingrained in him as practically not to exist for his consciousness at all.[1]

These habits create what I call "the freedom of discipline." When you discipline yourself to do something in a prescribed way—when you create standard work for yourself—you have greater freedom to think, create, and solve problems. Soldiers are better able to deal with the chaos and danger of actual battle because they don't have to think about where their ammunition is. Artists are better able to paint because they don't have to search for colors. Doctors can respond to emergencies faster because they don't have to think about the sequence of treatment steps. Far from shackling you to daily drudgery, standard work—that is to say, habits—free you to deploy all your creativity and intellect on the truly challenging and value-added work.

Habits are so cognitively beneficial because they obviate the need for conscious reasoning. Conscious thought resides in the prefrontal cortex of our brains, which is, unfortunately, quite limited—it can only process between four and nine variables at a time before becoming overburdened. As a result, our brains try to relegate as much processing as possible to the subconscious mind.

Standard work reduces the burden on the prefrontal cortex by forming routines that can be processed by the subconscious. This leaves the prefrontal cortex available for the kind of processing it does best when we really need it, such as dealing with novel circumstances or evaluating random information. In other words, just as Lean tools reduce waste and overburden in a physical process, they can reduce the waste and overburden in a psychological process as well.

Your work—whatever you do—has ample routine and repetitive tasks and processes that are ripe for creating standard work: processing e-mail, phone calls, filing, filling out expense reports, project management, presentations. Have you made these tasks routine, automatic, habitual? Or, do you need a rabbinical council for every minor activity? (Hmm, number 2 pencil or pen? Arial or Times New Roman? Leave the e-mail open on your computer or close it, mark it as unread, and hope you remember it—which, of course, preordains having to read it again?)

If you haven't relegated these tasks to habit, you're less efficient and productive than you could be, and that means you're not adding all the value you can to your organization or your customers. If you give yourself the freedom of discipline, you'll also give yourself the mental space to think, create, and innovate.

Mark's Story: Creating Order from Chaos

Mark is an emergency department (ED) physician. EDs use a five-level triage system to manage the inflow of patients. In this system, level 1 patients are those requiring immediate resuscitation. They automatically trump whatever else is going on when they arrive. Patients with complex conditions requiring many resources are level 2. Patients needing few or no resources occupy levels 4 and 5. Level 3 patients are somewhere in between. It often takes some effort to decide whether these patients are more like level 4/5 or level 2.

As part of their traditional standard work, the ED physician attends to the sickest patient first. This makes intuitive sense. After all, no one wants the sickest patients to wait longer than absolutely necessary. However, Mark noticed that it was most often the least ill—the level 4 and 5 patients—who backed up and clogged the flow of patients through the ED.

Mark engaged in PDCA to improve the process. He hypothesized (plan) that when there are many new patients to be seen at once, grouping together certain kinds of patients based on the complexity of the presenting complaint and the anticipated resource requirements would result in a faster overall throughput time for everyone in the ED.

He experimented (do) over several shifts by selecting charts in groups of three. He briefly visited a level 4 patient, like someone with an ankle sprain or urinary symptoms, who might need a single test. Next, he visited a level 2 patient with a straightforward presentation of symptoms to ensure that the initial appraisal was accurate and to confirm the appropriate initial testing. Last, Mark saw the level 3 patient, who required a fair bit of time to decide on the proper course of evaluation and treatment. At each stop, he charted just the unusual or positive findings since the remainder of the documentation required was straightforward and didn't require him to remember specifics. If the case were complicated, he stopped and did the chart at that moment to avoid forgetting important details.

By the time the initial circuit was complete, the level 4 patient's test would have come back, and Mark completed their visit. If it had been a level 5 patient, he finished their encounter without any testing at all. At that point, results for the level 2 patient would have returned, and he reviewed this patient's progress for additional treatment requirements. He also reviewed what other patients had arrived in the queue and which previously evaluated patient could be moved along to the next step. When Mark finished everything he could do at that time, he moved on to the next group of three patients.

In one typical shift, Mark received six cases at once. He started work on the first group of three patients within 15 minutes, then moved to the next group of three (not necessarily more complex, just three more of the mix). Within the first hour, he completed all the charting and discharged two of the more straightforward patients. Within 90 minutes, results were coming back, and he had completed the treatment plan on the others. There had also been two new patients arriving at the ED.

Reflecting back on the shift (check), Mark realized that his new process reduced the total time that patients were stuck in the ED. As he explained in his typically understated fashion, "Just like that, I had worked through the load of new cases and gotten caught up. What would have previously been a very stressful situation with six patients all arriving at once was reduced to a routine event by following my new procedure." And now, of course, he was free to continue with this new process (act) and make it his standardized work.

Mark was clear that this was not the only way, or "the right way," to prioritize work. This process works well for *him*, in the community hospital setting in which *he* works, usually as the only doctor on duty. A physician working in the acute side of a large ED, where all the patients are triaged as levels 1 and 2, would need a different approach. But by focusing on the entire value stream from the patient's perspective, applying PDCA, and creating standardized work for the new process, Mark has implemented successful kaizen.

Now, It's Your Turn: Step 1

Stop a moment and take a stab at defining standard work for a process in which you're involved. It could be performing credit checks on customers; closing the financial books each month; organizing the quarterly sales meeting; presenting the monthly department update to the executive team; or following up on action items from a meeting—whatever. Start small, with a process that's not too complex—you're not Hercules trying to clean up the Augean stable.

What are the steps involved in this process? List them in order. What common wastes (delays, errors, rework, overproduction) repeatedly crop up when you do this? What makes you think, "God, there's got to be a better way to do this!"

Hold on to this list. We will return to it shortly.

What Is Your Problem? Your Real Problem?

The whole idea of improvement—organizational or individual—rests on a crucial, if seldom discussed, point: You actually have to know what your problem is.

That sounds simple. It's not.

As high-achieving adults, we've spent our lives being rewarded for coming up with answers. Indeed, the faster you can come up with an answer, the more you're rewarded. The ability to come up with fast answers is the basis of pretty much every TV game show. It's a large part of your high school grades. It's probably even a factor in your performance evaluations at work. ("Bart does great work. He dives into problems and gets answers while other employees are just beginning to think about what to do.") Society rewards answers, not questions—notwithstanding the long-running success of *Jeopardy*.

The problem with this approach, however, is that we often jump to answers and solutions before we even know what the problem really is. As a result, the "solution" that we generate doesn't solve the problem at all; it's merely a Band-Aid on a symptom. It's a quick fix, fad diet ("Lose weight by eating only purple food!") approach that's not an improvement at all. It simply postpones the inevitable day of reckoning when you or the organization has to deal with the consequences of the real problem.

What's needed, then, is a way to identify the problems— the root causes—so that you can apply PDCA, create standard work, and make real improvements.

All manufacturing plants have a quality control group at the end of the production line. In a car factory, this group is responsible for buffing nicks in the paint, truing doors that don't close precisely, aligning mirrors, and so on. In traditional batch-and-queue plants, the production line never stops, even if the workers at a preceding point in the line see a problem. Management keeps the line moving at all costs and requires that the quality team fix any problems at the end. This is the quick-fix, Band-Aid approach to dealing with a problem.

By contrast, in a company that has embraced Lean, when a worker on the line spots a problem, he or she tries to fix the problem immediately, even stopping the line if necessary.

Rather than pass the error to the end of the line—where it will certainly be more expensive to fix and might be overlooked—the worker addresses the defect in real time. More importantly, the worker identifies the origin of the defect and creates a countermeasure to ensure that the problem never recurs. This is the root-cause approach to solving problems.

Which long-term system do you want?

Five Whys

One of the classic tools for getting to the root cause of a problem is the "five-why analysis." In this method, you ask a series of "why" questions until you identify the true underlying problem. The number five is just a guideline, though; you might only need three whys or you might need ten. The point is to get beyond simplistic, surface analysis so that you can really understand what is going on. When done properly, it's an incredibly powerful tool in uncovering the hidden problems that underlie the obvious symptoms. Indeed, Gary Convis, the former president of North American Toyota Motors Manufacturing, once said, "The vast majority of the improvements Toyota makes starts and finishes with a good 5-why."[2]

Jamie Flinchbaugh described[3] a five-why analysis well:

Why did the equipment fail?
  Because the circuit board burned out.
Why did the circuit board burn out?
  Because it overheated.
Why did it overheat?
  Because it wasn't getting enough air.
Why wasn't it getting enough air?
  Because the filter was clogged.
Why was the filter clogged?
  Because the filter wasn't changed.

Why wasn't the filter changed?
Because there was no preventive maintenance schedule.

And there you have it: The root cause of the equipment breakdown, in six whys. From this point, it's easy to develop a countermeasure—establish a preventive maintenance schedule—that solves the *real* problem.

It's worth pointing out that making this schedule is no guarantee of a permanent solution. You can easily imagine that in six months or two years, after a few changes in personnel and managers, that staff won't follow the preventive maintenance schedule. Then, you'd need to do another five-why analysis to figure out the root cause for people not following the schedule. The fact that there's no such thing as a permanent solution to a problem is why I like to use the term *countermeasure* rather than "solution."

Here's what a five-why analysis might look like for someone who works at a desk and suffers the consequences of continual interruptions and multitasking due to the flood of e-mail:

Why do I regularly miss important deadlines?
Because I'm always interrupted and can't get time to focus on my projects.
Why am I always interrupted?
Because most of our communication is via e-mail, and I have to stay on top of it every minute.
Why do you have to stay on top of e-mail?
Because sometimes there are urgent issues in e-mails that I have to deal with.
Why are urgent issues transmitted via e-mail?
Because it's fast and easy, and we don't use any other method.
Why don't you use any other method of communication?
Because we never established any rules for how to communicate urgent issues.

Ah—with this line of questioning, we've uncovered the real issue: The company crams every type of communication through one channel (e-mail) and has never considered using any other channel. That policy forces people to check their e-mail continually lest they miss something really big. Of course, those critical and urgent issues are few and far between, so 98% of the time the attention paid to e-mail isn't worth the cost of the interruption.

If you took a traditional time management approach to solving the problem of e-mail interruptions, you'd tell this person not to check e-mail so often. But, that kind of Band-Aid approach would fail here because it hasn't addressed the root cause of the problem. Our illustrative desk worker *has* to read every e-mail that comes in; after all, there really might be something urgent that must be dealt with now. The truth is that this person's behavior is totally rational under the current circumstances.

With the five-why analysis, however, we can create an effective countermeasure: for example, establish a policy that urgent issues that have to be handled within 10 minutes be communicated via pager, phone call, or text message. This policy gives the worker the security of knowing that nothing in his e-mail box needs immediate attention, and the worker can allow him- or herself to disengage from e-mail and focus on important project work. This countermeasure works because we're dealing with the root cause—undifferentiated communication channels—instead of the symptom—reading e-mail too often.

Your Turn: Step 2

Go back to the process that you mapped out and the problems you identified. Pick one problem and do a five-why analysis. Try to drill down to the root cause of the problem rather than getting distracted or stalled at the surface-level symptoms.

Obviously, I don't know what problem you are working on, so I can't give any feedback on your work. But, I can say that if your answer is, "Because we don't have enough money/people/time," you've gone down the wrong road. There's *never* enough money/people/time. Focus instead on the process: how and why is it done a certain way. That avenue of questioning is likely to be more fruitful.

Remember that a good five-why analysis is simple, but not easy. It requires the commitment to finding the root cause and the discipline to validate each why answer by checking it against the previous answer.

Implementing Improvement: A3 Thinking

Without a formal approach, an organization (or an individual) tends to be scattershot in improvement efforts. Some people take improvement seriously, and some just pay lip service to the idea of seeking continuous improvement. Some people are highly skilled in problem solving, and some struggle to distinguish between symptoms and root causes. What's needed is a standard approach to improvement. That's where the "A3 report" comes in.

The A3 report was developed by Toyota and is named for the international paper size on which it is written. (A3 paper is approximately ledger-size paper: 11 × 17 inches.) The report has a structured format that guides a person's improvement efforts in a rigorous and systematic way (Figure 5.3).

A3s typically include the following elements[4]:

- Title: Names the problem, theme, or issue.
- Owner/Date: Identifies who "owns" the problem or issue and the date of the latest revision.
- Background: Establishes the business context and importance of the issue.

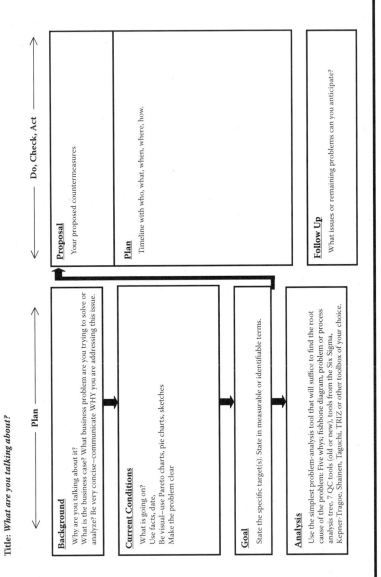

Title: *What are you talking about?*

Plan ────────────────►   ◄──────── Do, Check, Act ────────►

Background

Why are you talking about it?
What is the business case? What business problem are you trying to solve or analyze? Be very concise–communicate WHY you are addressing this issue.

Current Conditions

What is going on?
Use facts, date,
Be visual–use Pareto charts, pie charts, sketches
Make the problem clear

Goal

State the specific target(s). State in measurable or identifiable terms.

Analysis

Use the simplest problem-analysis tool that will suffice to find the root cause of the problem: Five whys; fishbone diagram, problem or process analysis tree, 7 QC tools (old or new), tools from the Six Sigma, Kepner-Tragoe, Shainen, Taguchi, TRIZ or other toolbox of your choice.

Proposal

Your proposed countermeasures

Plan

Timeline with who, what, when, where, how.

Follow Up

What issues or remaining problems can you anticipate?

Figure 5.3   A3 template.

- Current Conditions: Describes what's currently known about the problem or issue.
- Goals/Targets: Identifies the desired outcome.
- Analysis: Analyzes the situation and the underlying causes that have created the gap between the current situation and the desired outcome. This is where you can use your five-why analysis.
- Proposed Countermeasures: Proposes some corrective actions or countermeasures to address the problem, close the gap, or reach a goal.
- Plan: Prescribes an action plan of who will do what and by when in order to reach the goal.
- Follow-up: Creates a follow-up review/learning process and anticipates remaining issues.

The elements of the A3 follow each other in a logical sequence and are arranged so that the relationship between the problem, the root causes, the goal, the proposed counter-measures, and the methods for judging success are clear. But despite this structure, there is no "correct" template for an A3. It's not the format that matters, but the underlying thinking that leads people through the PDCA cycle.

The process of developing the A3—and I want to stress that it's the process that's important, not the act of condensing your thinking onto one piece of paper, no matter how large—is incredibly valuable. As John Shook explained in his book, *Managing to Learn*:

> Organizations can use A3 thinking to get decisions made, to achieve objectives and get things done, to align people and teams along common goals, and, above all, to learn for effectiveness, efficiency, and improvement. A3 works as both a problem-solving tools and as a structured process for creating prob-lem-solvers. The A3 helps spread a scientific method

that forces individuals to observe reality, present
data, propose a working countermeasure designed to
achieve the stated goal, and follow up with a process
of checking and adjusting for actual results.[5]

I won't go into much more detail about A3s because there
are several excellent books on the topic that deal with them
extensively.[6]

Of course, not every problem needs a full-blown A3. But
bringing the discipline of an A3 to your own improvement
efforts can be powerfully enlightening. Figure 5.4 is an A3
someone created because she was having difficulty making
progress on her assigned goals and objectives during a typical
workweek.

Another person created the A3 in Figure 5.5 to help him
improve his e-mail management. (The information technology
department at his company frequently suspended his e-mail
rights because of the size of his mailbox, which made his
daily work life difficult.)

Figure 5.6 is another A3 that deals with the difficulty of
tracking multiple action items and issues that require follow-
up in a complex office environment. This person analyzed the
flow of his work and the tools he used to identify a better way
to work.

Although these A3s are specific to each person's idiosyncratic work environment, my guess is that the fundamental issues they addressed are quite common, and that
you experience similar or identical problems, whether you
work alone or in a large company. The structured problem-
solving approach of the A3 can surely help you develop
effective countermeasures that can be deployed in your own
situation.

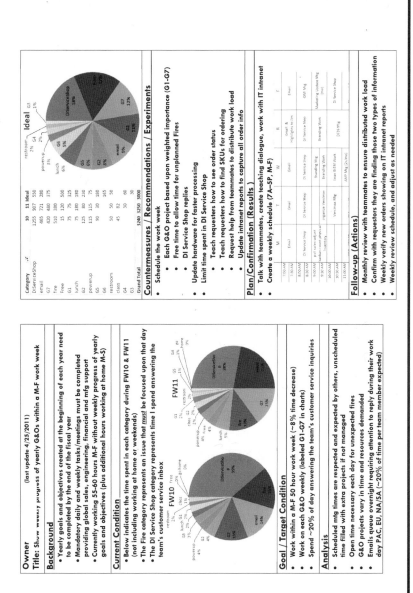

Figure 5.4   Goals and objectives A3.

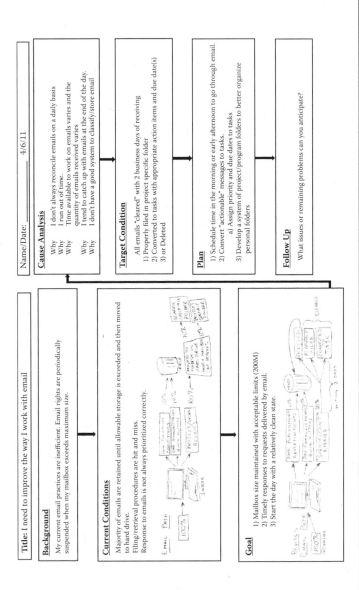

Title: I need to improve the way I work with email

Background

My current email practices are inefficient. Email rights are periodically suspended when my mailbox exceeds maximum size.

Current Conditions

Majority of emails are retained until allowable storage is exceeded and then moved to hard drive.
Filing/retrieval procedures are hit and miss.
Response to emails is not always prioritized correctly.

Goal

1) Mailbox size maintained with acceptable limits (200M)
2) Timely responses to requests delivered by email.
3) Start the day with a relatively clean state.

Name/Date: _____ 4/6/11

Cause Analysis

Why   I don't always reconcile emails on a daily basis
Why   I run out of time.
Why   Time available to work on emails varies and the
         quantity of emails received varies
Why   I tend to catch up with emails at the end of the day.
Why   I don't have a good system to classify/store email

Target Condition

All emails "cleared" with 2 business days of receiving
1) Properly filed in project specific folder
2) Converted to tasks with appropriate action items and due date(s)
3) or Deleted

Plan

1) Schedule time in the morning or early afternoon to go through email.
2) Convert "actionable" messages to tasks.
      a) Assign priority and due dates to tasks
3) Develop a system of project/program folders to better organize
      personal folders

Follow Up

What issues or remaining problems can you anticipate?

Figure 5.5   E-mail A3.

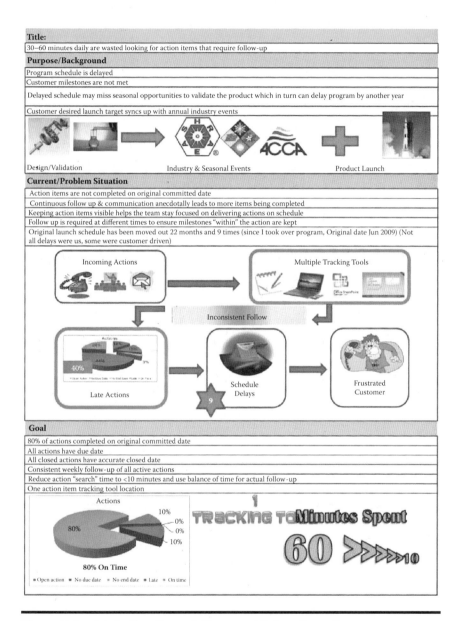

Figure 5.6 (a) Action items follow-up A3 (continued).

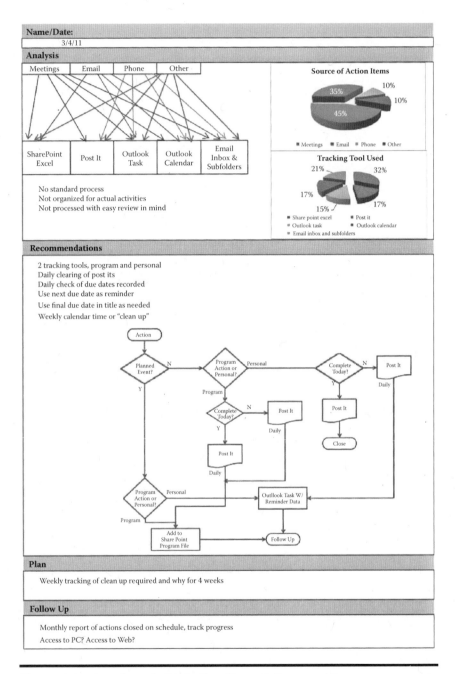

Figure 5.6 (continued) (b) Action items follow-up A3

Continuous Improvement

At the beginning of this chapter, I wrote that the work demands on your time and attention are virtually infinite and infinitely varied. How you organize your daily work will inevitably change from day to day.

If you view this ambiguity as inescapable, and the only appropriate response is to wing it, you'll have no ability to change and improve. Everything you do will be a one-off jazz riff—and you'd better hope you are really good at improvisation.

Alternatively, if your approach to the variability of your environment is to create rigid, inflexible responses ("That's the way I've always done it. That's the way it's always been done."), you've already become a fossil. You'll never be able to adapt to environmental changes, and you will never improve.

PDCA and standardized work, applied systematically with an A3, enable you to break out of both traps. You can bring (some) order to the chaos by creating standard work for predictable, routine, work. And once you have standard work, you can adapt to changes—or make your own changes—by using an A3 to systematically deploy PDCA. This process is a way to make best practice, common practice.

This is the ultimate goal of applying Lean tools at the individual level. It's not a quick fix, a short journey, or a fad diet. It's a way of learning to love your problems and challenges and to use them as a lever to discover ways of continuously improving. In today's global economy, more than ever, improvement is not optional. As General Eric Shinseki, the former chief of staff of the U.S. Army said, "If you don't like change, you're going to like irrelevance even less."

Notes

1. *The Principles of Psychology*, Volume 1, Williams James, Holt, New York, 1918, pp. 121–122 (accessed May 2, 2011, http://books.google.com/books?id=lbtE-xb5U-oC&dq=The%20 Principles%20of%20Psychology%2C%20volume%201%20 William%20James&pg=PA121#v=onepage&q&f=false).
2. As reported by Hal Macomber on his *Reforming Project Management* blog, http://www.reformingprojectmanagement. com/2009/06/01/991 (accessed April 24, 2011).
3. Adapted from *The Hitchhiker's Guide to Lean*, Jamie Flinchbaugh and Andy Carlino, Society of Manufacturing Engineers, Dearborn, MI, 2006, 20–21.
4. *Managing to Learn*, John Shook Lean Enterprise Institute, Cambridge, MA, 2008, 7.
5. Ibid., 4.
6. *Managing to Learn* by John Shook is one of them. Also see *Understanding A3 Thinking*, Productivity Press, Boca Raton, FL, 2008 by Durward Sobek and Art Smalley, and *The A3 Workbook*, Productivity Press, Boca Raton, FL, 2010 by Daniel Matthews.

Conclusion

"A factory of one."

I've developed this extended metaphor and coupled it with Lean concepts and tools in order to shift your thinking about how you work. I want you to rise above the muck and mire of your engorged inbox, and the frenzy of daily firefighting, so that you can reconsider not only what you're doing, but also how you're doing it.

There is a better way. You just need a method for improving it.

Jim Womack and Dan Jones once wrote that "most of the economic world, at any given time, is a brownfield of traditional activities performed in traditional ways."[1] I think this is true for the way that individuals work as well. Through technology we may have "paved the cow paths," but they're still cow paths. They aren't the superhighways that we really need to thrive and prosper in today's business environment. Developing those superhighways is a multistep process:

First, you must define the value you create—not the work you do, but the value you're actually delivering for your various customers.

Then, you need to be able to see the value as well as the waste in your environment. The tool of 5S helps you do this. And it helps you spot the problems while they're still small and inexpensive to fix.

Once you've cleared out the waste, how do you produce value in the shortest possible time? This is done by creating flow in your work, so that you're able to do your job most efficiently.

Of course, with all the projects you're managing and all competing commitments you're juggling, it's sometimes tough to know what to do next. Making your work visible helps you allocate your time and attention to the right work at the right time.

Finally, with the foundation for excellence laid, you can begin to do the really fun stuff: improving your own work processes with PDCA (plan, do, check, act) and standard work. At this level, you get to apply your creativity not only to the cool parts of your job but also to the way you do the job itself.

The great thing about this process is that you don't need top management support. You don't need a fat expense account, new equipment, or expensive software. You don't even need a corporate culture that's committed to improvement. You can work under a bunch of executive troglodytes in the white-collar equivalent of a salt mine and *still* apply these ideas. You only need your own commitment to improvement.

As I wrote this in 2011, the U.S. economy was finally starting to recover. New jobs were being added, but only slowly. People were still being asked to do jobs that were formerly done by two or three people. And with the fear of long-term unemployment vivid in everyone's minds, they've grimly adapted to the extra workload by getting to the office earlier, staying later, taking fewer holidays, and working more weekends.

Nowhere in that grim adaptation, however, is a structured approach for removing the waste in these jobs and improving the process by which they're performed.

But as a factory of one, you can make those improvements. And now is the best time to start.

Use the simple (but not necessarily easy) action steps I've included at the end of each chapter. Take a few—you don't need to do all of them at once—and try implementing them at work. Set new goals, track your progress, and celebrate your successes. Share your stories and your progress at http://www. afactoryofone.com. We'll have a community of like-minded adventurers there—including me—to provide feedback and coaching on your journey.

You can do this. Imagine your workdays filled with value and progress, instead of soul-sucking, mindless, and meaningless work. The power to make that change is yours.

Do it now.

Endnotes

1. Womack, James, and Daniel T. Jones, *Lean Thinking* (New York: Free Press, 2003), 28.

Index

Page numbers with an "n" refer to the notes at the end of the chapter.

About the Author

Daniel Markovitz is president of TimeBack Management (www.timebackmanagement.com), a consulting firm that radically improves individual and team performance by identifying and eliminating root cause impediments to productivity.

He is a faculty member at the Lean Enterprise Institute and teaches at the Stanford University Continuing Studies Program. He also leads a problem-solving workshop at the Ohio State University's Fisher School of Business.

Dan lived in Japan for four years and is fluent in Japanese. He's also an avid distance runner, an enthusiastic (but somewhat tentative) cyclist, and a determined (if slow) swimmer.

He holds an MBA from the Stanford University Graduate School of Business.

You can reach him at dan@timebackmanagement.com or via Twitter @timeback.